NETSUKE
Japanese Life and Legend in Miniature

NETSUKE
Japanese Life and Legend in Miniature

Edwin C. Symmes, Jr.

With a Foreword by HIH PRINCE NORIHITO OF TAKAMADO

TUTTLE PUBLISHING
Boston, Rutland, Vermont, Tokyo

The poem on page 162 is reprinted from An Introduction to Japanese Court Poetry, with translations by the author and Robert Brower, by Earl Miner, with the permission of the publisher, Stanford University Press: © 1968 by the Board of Trustees of the Leland Stanford Junior University.

The poems on pages 114 and 172 were translated by the editor, Stephen Comee.

I would especially like to thank my father, Ted Symmes, who has enthusiastically supported my photographic vision for forty years.

Published by Charles E. Tuttle Publishing, an imprint of Periplus (HK) Ltd.

LCC Card No. 89-517 14
ISBN 0-8048-2026-0

Book design, typography, and production art by Symmes Systems, Atlanta, Georgia.

First edition, 1991
First paperback edition, 1995
Fourth printing, 2000

Printed in Singapore

Distributed by:

USA
Tuttle Publishing
Distribution Center
Airport Industrial Park
364 Innovation Drive
North Clarendon,
VT 05759-9436
Tel: (802) 773 8930
Fax: (802) 773 6993

Japan
Tuttle Publishing
RK Bldg, 2nd Floor 2-13-10 Shimo-Meguro
Meguro-ku Tokyo 153 0064
Tel: (03) 5437 0171
Fax: (03) 5437 0755

Southeast Asia
Berkeley Books Pte Ltd
5 Little Road, #08-01
Singapore 536983
Tel: (65) 280 1330
Fax: (65) 280 6290

To my extraordinary wife

Rhena

Contents

List of Illustrations

Plate Number	Subject, *page*

Foreword

by HIH PRINCE NORIHITO OF TAKAMADO

Some time has passed since I was first bitten by the bug, and not only are there no signs whatsoever of my recovery, my condition actually seems to be getting worse by the day. When I first met her, my wife had already contracted the ailment, though I had no way of knowing that, and, needless to say, I was immediately infected. The disease caused by the Netsuke virus is indeed a serious malady. It sends strong roots deep into the hearts of its victims; it is incurable, even by the most radical methods; and it has spread and attached itself to carriers all over the world. In fact, so international has this veritable plague become that the number of patients afflicted with it in Japan is rather small in comparison with the thousands felled by it in other countries. The very book you are now holding is proof of the strength of the virus abroad. Beware, lest it capture you as well!

It is regrettable that many netsuke suffered the same fate as that of ukiyo-e—many of the best examples of now antique netsuke (and ukiyo-e) were carried abroad by foreign collectors. Yet, through an amazing twist of fate, it turned out to be this strong foreign interest that sustained the netsuke tradition and ensured its survival. Artists today create works that the most skilled craftsman could never have made in Edo-period Japan, and I am certain that the master carvers of the past are pleased with the achievements of their successors.

The qualities that I personally look for in a netsuke are warmth, wit, and a certain twist. Therein lies the reason that a netsuke is not simply a small sculpture. If the *inro* container with which it is worn is comparable to a Noh drama, the netsuke itself is a Kyogen play or a Kabuki piece. It is the amusing *senryu* or the satirical *kyoka*, rather than the more serious haiku or *tanka*. Small enough to be enclosed in the palm of the hand, a netsuke might be said to represent the ultimate in "artistic license." It always forces the viewer to discover what tale it wants to relate, what movement it wants to reveal, and what sounds it wants to make heard–all in a compact form that is round and warm to the touch.

Needless to say, the best way to appreciate a netsuke is to hold it, feel it, and examine it closely in one's hand. However, there is also much pleasure to be derived from studying good photographs of them. No matter how detailed a written explanation may be, it is no substitute for a good photograph. Books on netsuke without photographic illustrations are often extremely dull. But of the many illustrated books that I have seen, this is probably the first one in which the purpose of the photographs is more than just the recording of the details of each netsuke shown.

I have always been interested in photography. As a high-school student, I was an active member of the photography club and did my share of developing, enlarging, and experimenting. In fact, I was astounded when I first saw the quality of the photos in this book, because in one of my "experiments" I had placed sculptures in various surroundings and attempted to achieve a similar kind of effect. The specific settings in which Mr. Symmes has shot each netsuke both create fascinating photographs and focus on each netsuke with a completely new light. Each photograph is a perfect picture, and each netsuke springs to life and starts to speak. Mr. Symmes' approach in referring to various tales and proverbs, and in pointing out the significance of certain items and delving into many aspects of Japanese culture and tradition–all around the focal point of netsuke–is an amazing and excellent, not to mention enjoyable, one. It is an incredibly fresh approach and one that has never been attempted before.

I would like to express my appreciation to Mr. Symmes for having successfully realized such a novel idea. I sincerely hope that this book will help in bringing about a greater understanding not only of netsuke themselves but also of the Japanese culture that brought them into being and nurtured them for so long.

Preface
and
Acknowledgments

"Cute!" "Adorable!" "Incredible Craftsmanship!" "Tiny!" "Magnificent!" These are the comments heard whenever there is an exhibition of netsuke--the miniature carvings produced by highly specialized Japanese artists. More than just tiny objets d'art, they originally served the function of holding a pouch or set of nested boxes in place on a Japanese gentleman's pocket less clothing. This traditional use is explained in detail later.

This book is dedicated to the millions of people who have seen one of these fascinating carvings and wondered, "What is it?" I will attempt to answer that question, and provide a glimpse into the many facets of Japanese culture by enjoying some of the real and imaginary beings represented in these tiny yet powerful sculptures.

The Power of Netsuke

The influence that one netsuke can extend is something that continually amazes me. I have photographed hundreds of netsuke, not only for this book, but also for clients. Most of them are loaned to me just long enough to do the photograph and return the netsuke. Being an Asiaphile, I enjoy sharing these treasures with friends by showing them the ones that I am currently working on. Several years ago, I had photographed a nineteenth-century carving by Masatami of a mother monkey with two youngsters (page 16) for an advertisement. A friend that had seen many of the netsuke came into my studio and I showed it to her. With the first glance, tears welled up in her eyes. The tears flowed immediately and copiously. She could not explain why. Sobbing, she picked up the carving. I placed the carving out of sight and she calmed down.

About a year later, I was to be able to purchase a similar carving by the same artist. The same friend came into my studio shortly after I had acquired it.

While showing her another netsuke, I asked her if she would consider looking at a different carving by the same artist that had so moved her before. She agreed to look at it. Again, she had an immediate, deeply felt reaction to the carving. She cried until I took it away from her.

What is the power in that—or any—netsuke? How is such a small carving able to communicate so forcefully with someone who has little knowledge of Japanese culture, decades or even centuries after the carving was completed? Is it the same force that reaches out to the collector and makes them purchase a particular piece? Or is it different? Whatever the answer is, it seems that many netsuke have the power to influence people and pocketbooks. To paraphrase an advertisement, netsuke are like potato chips, "Nobody can collect just one!"

Multiple Meanings

The main purpose of this book is to introduce the fascinating world of Japanese culture, history, and folktales that comes to life through these special carvings. Each one has several interesting stories behind it. One story is usually obvious from the subject of the carving—such as the fly and the spider (Plate 6). However, there is usually at least one other story that is not readily seen by the average Western viewer. The Japanese viewer, or a Westerner who has studied Japanese culture, would recognize the folktale, legend, or historical incident that is alluded to by the subject matter of the netsuke.

One example of this multiple depth of meaning is the pine-cone netsuke (Plate 3). When seen by someone unfamiliar with the Japanese view of pine trees, it is just a charming, detailed carving of a pine cone. That is all that they might see in this 1 $7/8$ " long sculpture. Some people might associate the pine cone with memories of visiting a forest. A richly imaginative person might even remember the shape of a particular pine tree, the breeze he or she felt while lying under it, and the fresh smell of the mountain air. In much the same way, the Japanese viewers would relate their personal experiences to the object.

However, since many of the subjects carved in netsuke are also derived from traditional tales and legends, there is another layer of meanings for the Japanese.

This single pine cone is highly symbolic of long life. That is just one of the characteristics that the Japanese have associated with pine trees over the centuries. Also, since this is a closed pine cone, it still contains within it the seeds of future generations of pine trees. Therefore, the Japanese may interpret this as a symbol for renewing life, or youth. Traditionally, the pine tree is associated with bamboo and the plum tree. By inclusion, all of the stories associated with these plants are also brought to mind, just by viewing this simple carving of a single pine cone.

The netsuke shown in this book cover a broad spectrum—included are antique, semi-antique, and contemporary carvings, masterpieces and works by unknown carvers, and netsuke made from ivory, precious metals, and wood.

Yet, whether the carver is famous or not, whether the piece is ancient or not, whether the material is rare or not, or whether the image is pretty or not, every one of these images tells at least one story. Other variations and additional, related stories may be found in the books listed in the selected bibliography.

The names listed for the netsuke carvers are those supplied by the owners of the netsuke. Many of the netsuke shown here are from well-known collections and dealers, and should not require any additional verification. We believe that all information is as accurate as is possible.

The purpose of this book is to illuminate Japanese culture through photographs of netsuke with accompanying text.

Friends and Photography

The netsuke shown here were very generously loaned by friends and dealers to whom I am most grateful. The friends went without their "netsuke children" graciously—in one case, for over a year. The dealers patiently awaited the return of their stock and the return of sales. Without their dedicated assistance, impeccable taste, and commitment to quality, this book would have been far less interesting, if not impossible, to produce.

I must make special mention of my friend and client, Mr. Ralph deVille, owner of the Stone Lantern, an Oriental import shop in Highlands, North Carolina. I had already photographed many Japanese antiques for his ads when he shipped me a tiny carving of a man trimming a bonsai tree to be photographed. I prepared a suitable table-top space, used studio lighting to create an attractively graded tone background and photographed the netsuke. There were several others in the package, and all were photographed the same way.

When I delivered the photographs, Mr. deVille studied them in silence for quite a while. It felt like a very long time, since I was thinking that there was something he did not like about the images. Then he said, "Ed, these are the finest photographs I have ever seen of netsuke."

I felt a great relief.

Then he said, "But they are so plain. Can't you do *something* to make them *more interesting?*"

If you ever have a chance to visit the Stone Lantern, you will understand his question, as it is filled to the brim with wonderful Oriental treasures.

I returned to the studio and re-photographed the bonsai master in a miniature scene that I created with pine branches. We used the photograph full page, in full color for his advertisement. That image was the catalyst that sparked the creation of miniature settings for the netsuke that are included in this book.

Mr. deVille is also responsible for loaning many of the netsuke that appear in this book, either directly from his stock, or indirectly by introducing me to netsuke collectors with a superb sense of quality.

Although we both have lived in Massachusetts, it was only through producing this book that I met Stephen Comee in Tokyo, Japan. He has provided sensitive and creative assistance as the editor of this book through the Charles E. Tuttle Company.

Our friends in Japan, Bill and Sayoko Holt, made our trip to Kumamoto delightful, and arranged countless details to facilitate our incredibly tight time schedule. We also appreciate Bill's colleague, Ogata Sensei, arranging our tour of the Kumamoto Handicrafts Center, just one among many kindnesses that he and all of the thoughtful neighbors extended to us in Kumamoto.

For taking care of our physical and spiritual needs in Tokyo, we especially appreciate Hideharu Onuma Sensei, my Kyudo Master. Our trips to Tokyo would not have been possible without the helpfulness that he repeatedly extended personally and through his assistant, Dan DeProspero, who is the only American ever to be certified to teach kyudo by the All Japan Kyudo Federation.

The photographs in this book were conceived and created over an eight-year period. Of course, the actual work was not full time, but the ideas were always at the fore-front of my thinking. Just finding props that were small enough to be in scale with the netsuke was an on-going and interesting project. Setting up the scene and then lighting it properly could take from a couple of hours to a full day. Even the film exposure was tedious, taking as long as 6 minutes for each sheet of 4" x 5" film. Most of the photography was done between 10:00 P.M. and 3:00 A.M. This time schedule was dictated by trying to work this project in between work and family duties. It also helped assure that there would be no interruptions during the set up and photography because security was a major consideration. Some of these netsuke could cost more than a new car if damaged or stolen. Many of the details are included in the section, *Notes on Photographing Netsuke,* (Page 38).

I also wish to include a note of appreciation to Mark Gresham for helping me through the maze of computer-generated invisible gremlins so that I could accomplish writing this book. Another computer assist came from Jan Isley, who upgraded the inner workings of my ancient computer so that it would conveniently handle this book-length manuscript. More importantly, he discovered the secret of how to restore all of my files when we thought that the whole manuscript file had been stolen by the above-mentioned computer gremlins.

Thanks to Rodney Grantham, a friend of some 20 years and a dealer and consultant on ukiyo-e for the, at times, long-term loans from his extensive library on topics Japanese. Appreciation is also due to Michael Spindel, who has taken on the responsibility of marketing contemporary netsuke in America. He has provided many helpful suggestions and much information on contemporary netsuke master carvers.

I owe a great deal of my understanding of Japanese culture to the bonsai master, Yuji Yoshimura, with whom I have worked intimately on two previous books. His life is a continuing example of what one person can do to positively influence others.

The concept of this book is dedicated to all people who wish to know more about cultures other than their own. The physical presence of this book is dedicated to my wife, Rhena, for it was only with her complete understanding and total support, that this book was able to come to fruition.

All of the efforts to create this book for the past decade will have been worthwhile if it answers some of the questions that you may have had about Japanese life and legend. It is my hope that it will also create an interest in learning more about Japan and Japanese culture.

EDWIN C. SYMMES, JR.

A Guide to the
Pronounciation of Japanese

Vowels

The pronunciation of Japanese is fairly simple. The Japanese language has five vowels, *a, i, u, e,* and *o,* which are pronounced as follows:

a	as in f*a*ther
i	as in *i*nk
u	as in J*u*ne, but shorter
e	as in p*e*t
o	as in s*o*

Note that in spoken Japanese, the vowels *i* and *u* are often elided (omitted or slurred) as in the words *shika* (deer) and *desu* (is), which sound like *sh'ka* and *des'.*

Long vowels are not indicated in this text.

Consonants

Most consonants are pronounced as in English, with the exception of the Japanese *r* and *n*.

The Japanese *r* is closer to the English *l* sound, and even closer to the British flipped *r* as in their pronunciation of *very*, which sounds almost like *veddy* to Americans.

The Japanese *n* is also different, being always slightly nasalized, except when it appears as the first letter of a word or new syllable.

Double consonants (*kk, ss, ssh, tt, tch, tts,* and *pp*) are pronounced much like double consonants in Italian, where each one is pronounced, as in *vendetta.*

Nikko---a famous tourist town	as in boo*kk*eeper
issei---a generation	as in le*ss s*leep
issho---together	as in po*sh sh*op
kitte---a stamp	as in ho*t t*ub
matchi---a match	as in ha*t ch*eck
ittsu---one letter	as in fa*t ts*ar
rippa---splendid	as in to*p p*art

All other sounds should be pronounced as in English, or as in Italian.

Introduction

The range of objects that are called netsuke is tremendous—from natural rocks, shells, and roots to simple carvings. They also include simply elegant masterworks and even modern trinket-netsuke. Each object qualifies as a netsuke. Each one is different. Therefore, it is almost a universal statement that anyone can find a netsuke that he likes. No matter what your taste is in design, materials, subject, colors, textures, or time period, there is a netsuke out there just waiting for you to discover it. Discover one that you love, and the whole world of Japanese art, legends, and life will open a new door for you.

Ojime, the little beads that hold the *inro* cords taut at the top of the case, comprise an entire collectible art field in themselves. They come in as many materials and styles as do netsuke, because all of the requirements are the same. They must be hard enough to stand up to wear, they must hold fine detail when carved, and they must have a pleasant feel to the hand.

The simplest *ojime* is just a tiny ball with a hole through it. Some ball shaped *ojime* are carved in bas relief such as the 10,000 chrysanthemum design. The ivory carving of an archer has such fine detail that even the bow string is carved in relief. The ripe peach adds a protruding element—the leaf and stem to add interest to the simple bead shape. This ivory carving has been lacquered to give it a more realistic appearance.

Each of these styles has its attributes, but the carving of the dog and the dragon in full relief is a supreme example of the *ojime* carver's skill. The entire composition is realized within a sphere that is only $5/8$" in diameter.

What Is a Netsuke?

The two Japanese characters that are used to spell the word "netsuke" are *ne,* which means "root," such as a wisteria or bamboo root that might have been used as an early netsuke, and *tsuke,* which means "to fasten." Thus, netsuke originally meant a root that had been fastened to something.

In other texts, a netsuke is usually referred to by the English word "toggle." The dictionary definition is appropriate–"a device used to secure or hold something, especially: a. a pin inserted in a nautical knot to keep it from slipping; b. a device attached to the end of or inserted in a loop in a rope, chain, or strap to prevent slipping, to tighten or to hold an attached object." Yet it seems that common usage of the word "toggle" is more aligned with "toggle bolt" or "toggle switch," and thus leans away from the meaning of a "device attached to the end of a rope to keep it from slipping." Therefore, instead of using any English synonym, the word netsuke will be used in this book.

The first netsuke was probably invented by an enterprising Japanese who needed to carry some small personal items such as money and herbs with him. Westerners would have put the money in their wallet or purses and the herbs in an envelope in their pocket. The Japanese, of course, couldn't do that, because they had no pockets in their kimonos.

A basket or pouch may have been the first useful way of carrying objects. But they had to be held. And carrying something in one hand not only hampers your swordsmanship, it is inconvenient and tiring. Thus, smaller baskets and pouches were made that could be tied to the belt of the kimono, called an *obi*, with a cord. Then someone discovered that he could tie a stick or attractive root to the free end of the cord and slide the stick upward under the *obi* and let it hang out from the top.

When the basket pulled down on the cord, it snugged the root into the top edge of the *obi* and kept the cord from pulling back through. Whenever the wearer wanted to look into the basket, he could just slide the stick out from under the *obi* and have everything within easy reach.

Netsuke were also traditionally used for carrying a purse, tobacco pouch, pipe-case, or anything else that might be suspended from the *obi* in addition to the *inro* (see below).

Being creative, artistic people, someone carved the stick to make it more attractive. The single compartment basket was soon divided into many smaller sections to allow for easier access to the contents. The stick then became the netsuke, and the basket came to be known as an *inro*. Each of these items has developed into an art form of its own. It is interesting to note that netsuke have become so popular today that modern netsuke carvers are kept busy producing their own masterworks, even though most Japanese wear Western-style clothing with pockets. Modern netsuke are collected as artworks by connoisseurs; they are almost never put into everyday use anymore.

As the *inro* and netsuke were refined, they began to be crafted out of more elegant materials. *Inro* are frequently made by coating a nest of wooden boxes with dozens upon dozens of coats of lacquer. The craftsmanship is so incredible that, when all of the boxes are fitted together, the scene on the outside seems to be continuous. Yet it may actually go over 5 to 7 seams within the 4-inch length of the box (see photographs on opposite page). To hold each of these sections together, a channel was designed into the outside edges of the boxes to hold a cord. This channel eventually was enclosed so that the cord passed through, invisible to the eye and not disturbing the beautiful design on the exterior.

Where the cord emerges from the top edge of the *inro*, the two strands must be pulled together to hold the box sections tightly in place. The cords are passed through a small bead that can be moved up and down to tighten or loosen the row of boxes. This bead is called an *ojime*.

The cords then go up to the netsuke. Once the netsuke became more than a natural object, some method of attaching the cords was required. Most netsuke have a pair of holes, connected by a tunnel, usually in the back of the carving, so that the cord may be passed through it. Usually, one hole is larger than the other so that the knot can be concealed within the netsuke. This pair of connected holes is called the *himotoshi*. Some clever carvers devised natural ways for the cord to be attached, such as going between the nuts of the ginkgo cluster shown in Plate 9.

This exquisite lacquer *inro* was created in the late seventeenth century by the artist Jokasai. It measures 2 ¹³/₁₆" long and has the original gold lacquered *ojime* with it. The netsuke is described in Plate 17.

This photograph shows how *inro* were created to facilitate carrying different items in the multiple boxes. Notice the beautiful lacquerwork even on the interior of the boxes.

Bottom, Left The incredible quality of the craftsmanship is shown here by following the design across the almost imperceptible gaps between boxes.

Bottom, Right The *himotoshi* is a tunnel carved into the netsuke to allow a cord to be fastened to it. It is usually in the back or bottom of the netsuke which thus faces the viewer when in use.

The panels of the left column show, respectively, contemporary carvings, famous Japanese legends, "trick" netsuke and a European carving. The photographs below show several views of one netsuke to illustrate the carver's attention to even the smallest details.

The stick, now transformed into a netsuke; the bead or *ojime;* and the nest of boxes, or *inro* make up a set (*see* page 27 plus Frontispiece and Plate 1). The techniques and skills necessary for producing a lacquer *inro* are quite different from those required for carving a netsuke. So usually, even though the subject matter may be coordinated, the pieces were produced by different artists. And this could be an interesting pastime for the buyer—coordinating netsuke, *ojime*, and *inro* by different artists to make a set of their own choosing. Of course, there were some artists that were able to produce the entire set, and such rare sets have always been greatly treasured.

In bringing a set together, one person might choose to have all of the elements showing the same subject, such as turtles—a symbol of long life. One turtle may be shown floating on a log, all lacquered onto the *inro.* The *ojime* may be a single carved turtle, and the netsuke might be a whole pile of turtles, with the cord passing between two of them. Another person may decide to match the same turtle *inro* with an *ojime* of a pine cone and a netsuke of a crane. Why? Because the turtle, pine, and crane are all traditional Japanese symbols of long life.

The meaning of symbols is very important to the Japanese. Their written language was devised from symbols representing objects. Symbols are basic to the Japanese culture and all symbols relate to some aspect of the object they are connected with. Cranes, for instance represent fidelity because they mate for life. An object decorated with cranes is considered to be an excellent wedding gift. Westerners would appreciate the beautiful design, but the Japanese would also understand the thoughtfulness of the symbolism that it represents.

These symbols are fascinating to study. They are fun. Not all are happy, but most are based upon some captivating story—real or imagined—about the subject. And it is knowledge of these stories that we in the West are often missing when we see beautiful objects from Japan.

Netsuke are one of the richest sources of Japanese stories. Almost every piece that has ever been carved has a story to go with it. Sometimes the netsuke is based upon a legend or folktale (Plate 7). Sometimes, it has to do with the characteristics of the subject itself (Plate 47). Sometimes, it may be about the material that it is made from (Plate 26), or it can be about the artist himself (Plate 65).

Throughout *Netsuke: Japanese Life and Legend in Miniature,* you will meet the legends, the stories, and the people that make up the extraordinarily rich artistic heritage of the Japanese.

# Netsuke Carving

Notes on Netsuke Carving

Netsuke have been created from almost every imaginable material. As mentioned earlier, objects such as roots, stones, and sea shells have been utilized successfully. In those, the only "creative" aspect was to find something attractive and tie the cord to it. Some netsuke are made from lacquer, a process of building up the form with repeated coats of lacquer paint (*see* Plate 67). Another group of materials used is ceramics. With these, the form is modeled in clay; it is then fired in a kiln to harden it. Subsequent firings with glazes can be done to give additional colors to the netsuke (Plate 35). Metalworkers created many netsuke. Some are done entirely of metal, and others use metalwork as an accent such as the spider resting on the wooden mushrooms in Plate 17.

The majority were created by carving. And what exquisite carvings they are! It is fairly safe to say that there is no suitable material that has not been carved to create netsuke. Although ivory and boxwood have been two traditional favorite materials, everything from mammoth tusk to pine has also been used. In fact, many netsuke use more than one material. Some use the additional material naturally such as an ebony figure of a South Seas diver clutching a natural piece of coral. A frequently used second material is horn, which is often inset to give the eyes a translucent glow that heightens the liveliness of the carving.

With many nations honoring the ban on international trade in ivory, the netsuke carvers have been seeking new and/or different materials to work in. They have been searching for material that is as strong as ivory and will hold the crispness of detail in the carvings that ivory is noted for. In looking for a material that is acceptable to the conservationists, even synthetic materials have been used in experiments. Fortunately, collectors of fine netsuke are interested in the art form, not merely ivory carvings. The result has been an increase in the variety of materials that are currently used by netsuke carvers.

Two examples of new materials for netsuke carving are mammoth tusk (Plate 5), and hippopotamus tooth (page 36). Other materials include pink ivory wood from New Zealand, mountain mahogany from the United States, and fossilized walrus tusk. These natural materials and many others now provide a richer palette from which the netsuke carver can choose to create a particular effect. The master carver will always choose to imbue his ideas, spirit, and designs into the rich, compelling beauty of natural materials.

Contrary to the original fear that the ivory embargo would eliminate netsuke carving, it has infused a new vigor into the carvers as they learn to work with and master the variety of materials available to them today. And this in turn gives the netsuke collector a greater range of beautiful objects from which to choose.

Katsutoshi Saito carves under the artist's name of Bishu. When my editor, Stephen Comee, and I visited him at his home/studio on the outskirts of Tokyo, he was happy to welcome us into his carving studio. Bishu is the president of the International Netsuke Carvers' Association, and was instrumental in getting members to change the former name of the Japan Netsuke Carvers' Association to reflect the international interest in netsuke and netsuke carving. One might think that he is a radical for encouraging non-Japanese to carve netsuke. However, as we found on our visit, he is a charming, gracious host who freely answered all of our questions and posed for what must have seemed like endless photographs.

Bishu is a fourth-generation carver. His feelings for the traditions of ivory carving are strong. Yet he is a contemporary artist and his designs have an unmistakable quality to them not found in the work of the carvers from previous generations. His grandfather established a carving workshop that his father also continued. However, rather than turn out production work, Bishu chose to create only one-of-a-kind netsuke and closed down the workshop.

Looking at his work, holding it, feeling the spirit of the carver being imparted through a supposedly inanimate object, is quite a revelation. He is a man of the late twentieth century, but his creativity seems to come from an older culture, one where time was

not of the essence. Bishu's netsuke come from a period when brilliance of concept and quality of execution, rather than mass production of low-cost items, were the most important criteria.

Each traditional netsuke carver creates his own tools. They must be right for his style of carving and be comfortable for the way that he carves. Although the term generally used is "carving", a term that better describes most of the process is really "scraping." One of the few concessions to modern equipment is a power grinder that Bishu uses to sharpen his hand carving tools.

The ban on international shipment of ivory has created many problems in Japan, since there are several traditional arts that depend upon a steady supply of ivory. Netsuke carving is just one of them and used only about 2% of the total volume. Bishu has researched hundreds of different materials to find a suitable substitute for ivory. It is not easy to find one, because the material must be hard enough to take handling well, fine-grained enough to hold a sharp carved edge, be workable with traditional equipment, have a pleasing feel and look to it. For some netsuke, it must also accept lacquer, metals, and inlays of other materials.

During our interview, Bishu revealed that he has found a material that he believes is actually superior to elephant ivory. It is nearly identical to ivory in working characteristics, but it is actually a little bit harder than ivory, so that it allows finer detail. Plus, it is acceptable to the conservationists. He showed us many of the materials that he had tried—boxwood, walrus tusks from Siberia, frozen mammoth tusks, mahogany, and even a bone from the penis of a whale. The photograph at left shows all of these, plus the new material—hippopotamus tooth. The cause for celebration is that hippopotamuses in captivity must have their teeth cut off periodically because they are not worn down as in nature.

Mammoth ivory is another excellent "new" material. It carves almost exactly like elephant ivory, but also has subtle colorations incorporated into it from the minerals that it has absorbed over the tens of thousands of years that it has been buried. Fine quality mammoth ivory is extremely rare, but is still found in Siberia and in Alaska. Since mammoth ivory looks very similar to elephant ivory, international customs officials have developed positive identification tests for this material.

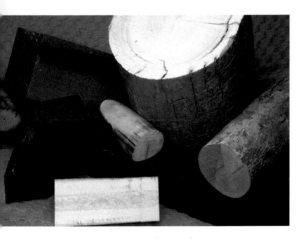

Clockwise from the top: mammoth ivory, boxwood, ebony, fossil walrus tusk, mahogany, bone from the penis of a whale, rosewood, and center, hippopotamus tooth.

34

The accompanying photographs show Bishu at work in his studio just outside of Tokyo, Japan.

Seated in the manner of a traditional craftsman, Bishu works six to eight hours a day carving netsuke (c). He said that he had tried carving at a table but that the posture was difficult and he got tired easily. By sitting on the floor, he carves with energy from his whole body, rather than just from his hands.

a

The choice of materials can depend upon the subject as well as upon the carver's interest at the moment. Many traditional netsuke carvers specialized in one material, but the contemporary netsuke carver must be able to realize his creation in many different materials.

b

Although modern power tools are available to contemporary netsuke carvers, they still rely on traditional tools. One reason is that they enjoy working with the material. When using the traditional tools to scrape and drill, the object being created is being liberated by a living, creative force. It is imbued with the energy and the spirit of the master carver. Power tools create an interface—a distance between the creator and the object. They may allow impressive technical accomplishments to be produced faster, but they block the spirit of the master carver from penetrating the netsuke.

Bishu likes to work in simple geometric shapes. He has a series of plaster models that he studies to see how a new creation will harmonize with the basic shape such as this ball (a).

c

Often, he will sketch the subject onto the basic geometric shape. This sphere (b) shows the beginnings of one of his sensuous rabbits.

When he was seventeen years old, Bishu began learning the techniques of ivory carving from his father. Many things have changed since then but the carving techniques are still the same (d). Electric lighting and stereo sound seem to be the only differences between Bishu's techniques today and those of the master carvers two centuries ago.

d

Now we can see how the visualization and the completion are united. This sensuous rabbit (e) is a netsuke that Bishu created in 1977. It is still in his collection, rather than having been sold because it developed a slight crack while he was working on it. He would not sell the "defective" piece. He uses it frequently, though, and in a very traditional manner. He puts his cigarettes into a pouch that is attached to the netsuke and then

e

slides the netsuke under his belt. This arrangement allows him to carry the cigarettes without crushing them in today's tight-fitting jeans.

The photograph at left shows a hippopotamus tooth and the netsuke that Bishu created from a section of it. We wonder what intriguing image he may find within the other sections of the tooth that still remain, awaiting his master-touch.

Another Bishu creation is *A Fable from Chuang-tzu,* shown at left. In this netsuke, he has used an ancient Chinese tale as the inspiration to combine two natural animals and a supernatural creature into one fabulous netsuke. In the Chinese fable, the sage Chuang-tzu went to visit the ruler of the kingdom of Liang. The ruler, Hui Shih, who had seized his throne by force, was afraid that he was about to be overthrown, and ordered his armies to stop Chuang-tzu. They couldn't even find him. When Chuang-tzu arrived anyway, he said to Hui Shih: "The phoenix is said to fly from the great southern ocean to the northern sea, stopping to rest only in the sacred dryandra tree. It eats only the tenderest bamboo shoots, and drinks only from the purest springs. As it happened to pass over an owl that had seized a decaying rat, the owl looked up and, seeing the mighty phoenix, trembled in fear that his meal might be stolen. The owl let out a loud hoot.

"Are you trying to hoot me out of Liang?", he concluded.

Bishu says that each fine netsuke should be viewed as a precious work of art that emerges today from a four-hundred-year-old tradition. Yes, each piece is a sculpture, but it is a sculpture that is peculiar to Japan and inextricably linked with Japanese culture and tradition. His ideal, as is our intention in producing this book, is to create a greater understanding of Japanese culture throughout the world. Therefore, he was one of the first netsuke carvers to accept a non-Japanese student.

In addition, he has spoken to international netsuke collectors in private and at conventions. In late 1989, there were 42 members of the International Netsuke Carvers' Association. Nearly all of the members under 40 years of age are Westerners.

Advice to an aspiring carver from the master is: "If you don't do it every day, all day

Photograph courtesy of the owner.

long, you are never going to master carving netsuke."

Bishu's advice for the beginning (or advanced) collector is, "First, you must look at the netsuke at a distance. At least at arm's length. Then if you like the shape from that distance, bring it a little closer so that you can see more of what it is. Finally, study it close up so that you can enjoy the technique." He says that many people buy a particular netsuke only for technique. If it is not also a fine work of art, they tire of it easily.

a

As mentioned previously, not all netsuke are created by carving. Some are woven, some are molded or sculpted in clay or porcelain. Others are made from metal. It is comparatively easy to understand that a netsuke could be carved from a piece of wood, but the idea of creating one by carving and inlaying metals, seems most difficult.

Japanese metalwork is world renowned– especially in swords. In peaceful times, metalworkers turned to more decorative objects, netsuke among them. On the southern island of Kyushu, there is a traditional form of metalwork that is most interesting.

The overall shape is created and then the surface of the piece is roughed up by hammering row after nearly imperceptible row of troughs and ridges (b) into the metal surface. The tools for working metal are quite different (a) from those used in carving wood or ivory . The next step is to lay gold or silver wire into place and pound it with an ivory peg until it joins with the base metal. This technique allows for extremely delicate designs and lends it self to art nouveau–like designs of intertwining vines and flowers (c).

b

c

The finished piece may then be mounted in an ivory disc to form a *kagami-buta style* netsuke or may even be a free-form *ojime.*

This metalwork as well as knife making and many other traditional arts, are being preserved by the Kumamoto Handicrafts Center on Kyushu. There is a full exhibition area of historical crafts as well as a large shopping area that is a merchandising outlet for traditional craftsmen. The center alleviates the marketing aspect for the artist and greatly reduces the problems associated with running a small business. It is located across the street from the imposing Kumamoto castle, a must-see location for anyone visiting southern Japan.

Kumamoto Castle

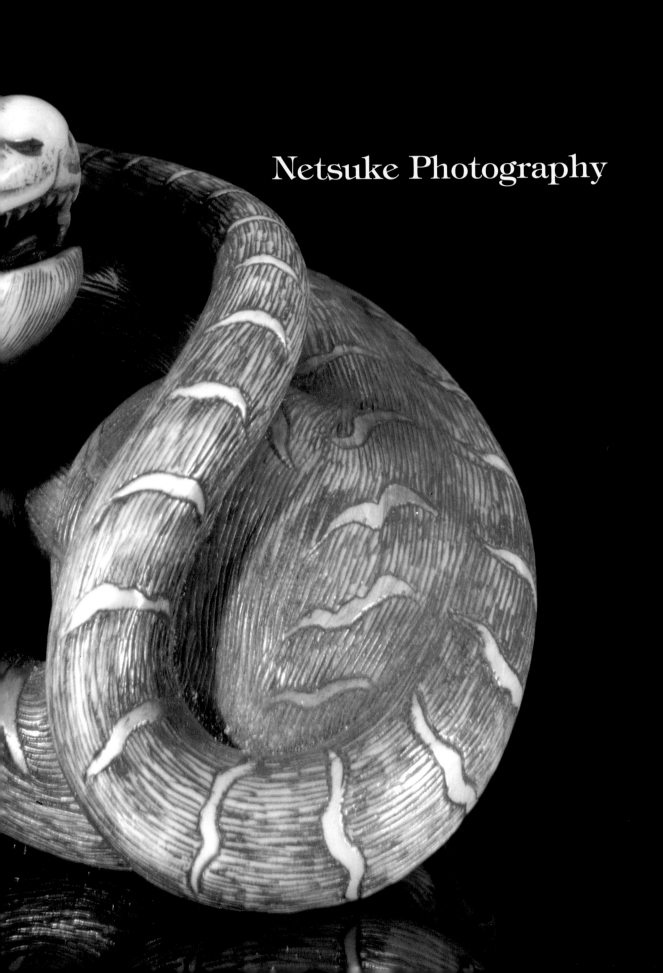

Netsuke Photography

Notes on Netsuke Photography

Before we look at the technical and aesthetic aspects of how to photograph netsuke, there is one main question that must be answered.

"What is your purpose in photographing these netsuke?"

The reason that this is such an important question is that the equipment required will vary greatly depending upon the final use of the photographs. And that variation is what can stretch your pocketbook into a second mortgage.

In the least complicated/expensive department, the answer might be, "To remind me what I have in my safe deposit box." In this case, the image that is required can be captured with a Polaroid instant camera that allows close focusing. The camera does the exposure automatically, and some are even able to focus close-up automatically too.

The next most complicated answer is, "In case I need to show my insurance agency."

One of the biggest problems in photographing netsuke is that they are so small. Inexpensive, ordinary cameras do not allow you to focus close enough to capture an image that will be more than a pencil eraser sized blob on your print. That type of tiny, fuzzy image is not aesthetically pleasing, and is not acceptable for insurance purposes either. One option that is now available for insurance purposes is to use a video camcorder. Most units incorporate a "macro" setting. This feature will allow you to focus closely enough to nearly fill the screen with your netsuke. The focusing may be manual at that distance, but the exposure will be automatic. A video tape stored in a safe location is acceptable proof for an insurance company if anything should happen to your home.

Most advanced still cameras allow you to use interchangeable lenses. Any system like that will take a "macro" or close-focusing lenses. With that type of lens and a 35mm camera, you can get good quality images even from a one-hour photo processor.

However, if your answer is, "I want to have my photographs published!", then there are many other considerations. Film size, film type, method of lighting, and photographic situations all become important variables. For the moment, let's assume that all you need is a good clean image for insurance purposes.

Arranging lighting is usually a difficult aspect of photography for the amateur. If they have any lighting equipment at all, it is usually a small electronic flash. These units emit a bright light from a small flash tube. They produce a very harsh light which is not usually what we need to photograph netsuke. Flood lights may be used, but you will be limited to using "Tungsten" type slide film. There is no print film that is color corrected for flood lights. Taking a negative exposed under flood lights to a fast-service photo lab is a sure recipe for bad color–green ivory, or perhaps it will be purplish, or even tinted golden.

The reason is that most film is made to be exposed by sunlight. Electronic flash is the same color as sunlight, so the film remains the proper color with flash exposure. However, when we take pictures with flood lights or in ordinary room lights, whether they are "bulbs" or fluorescent tubes, there is a difference in the color of the light illuminating the subject. That color difference will be recorded on the film. Most color print processing machines are set up to analyze skin tones and set a proper color balance for the print. Our netsuke photographs will have colors that the machines are not familiar with, and therefore, the machine is unable to set the proper color balance for our prints.

One easy solution is to buy a piece of neutral grey cloth such as silk or felt. Then take the cloth outside and put it in a pile on top of your car. The hood, trunk or roof will do. Now move around so that the sun is coming over your left shoulder, or is as high and from the left as possible. Smooth out an area in the front of the cloth and make sure that there is a mound behind it tall enough to cover up any background scenes that will distract from your netsuke.

Place the netsuke on the flat area of the cloth and enjoy photographing it in natural sunlight. Get as close as possible so that the image is as large as possible and still be in focus in your view finder. If you have an automatic exposure camera, you will not have to worry about the exposure as long as you have chosen a medium tone for the cloth. Be sure to take photographs of the front and back and of the signature if your camera will focus that closely.

There is one technical consideration that you should be aware of–there is a direct relationship between the size of the lens opening and the distance, front to back, that will be in sharp focus.

Experienced photographers already know what to do and why. For everyone else, the easy way to remember this is to set your camera at the largest number possible for the lens opening that will still give you an acceptable exposure (an f-stop of f/16 is much, much better than one of f/4). When you are photographing something very small like a netsuke, the band that is in focus can be as narrow as 1/4 inch. By using a larger number, the whole netsuke can be pulled into focus.

In automatic exposure cameras, the metering system chooses a lens opening and a shutter speed that will produce the proper exposure for the scene that the meter is pointing at. You can help it choose the lens opening that you want by selecting the slowest shutter speed at which you can hold the camera still. This will probably be 1/60 or 1/125 of a second. If you use a faster shutter, the camera will choose a lens opening that will give you less area in focus.

There are some film considerations that could take a whole book to amplify and illustrate. But they too, can be simplified to a single statement--use the slowest ASA film possible.

There have been many changes in films in the past 35 years since I began taking photographs. The fast films available today are truly incredible feats of engineering and deliver an excellent image, especially when compared to the older films. But the slower the ASA rating is on the film, the more detail it will record. Period.

Whether you choose to make slides or prints is your preference. There is no such thing as a permanent color photograph. So if you want an image that will last for your lifetime, take it on black and white film, and then have it processed properly. Color transparencies will fade. Color negatives will fade. Color prints will fade. Even electronic imaging such as video tape has some problems with long-term storage. Store your photographs in cool, relatively normal humidity conditions like a first-floor closet. Never put them in the basement or attic.

Professional Photography

When I began this project, I wanted the images to reproduce as beautifully as possible, so I chose to photograph everything with a studio camera that makes an image that is 4" x 5" in size. This gives the printing production companies the best detail to work with. It also created a lot of photographic problems.

One example is that many of the images required as much of the image being in focus as possible.

This requirement forced me to use a very small lens opening. The smallest lens opening on most cameras is f/16 or f/22. I used a lens for some of these images with an opening of f/128. That means that the exposure time was very long. For instance, if a correct exposure was one second at f/16, it would take sixty-four seconds at f/128. Some of the exposures were as long as seven minutes. At that length of exposure, film does not react to light in the same way that it does at exposures of less than five seconds. This is called reciprocity. It changes the color balance of the film and the sensitivity to light. To re-color balance the film, filters must be used in the camera.

To calculate the exposure, several variables must be taken into account. The first is the speed of the film. The second is the amount of light falling on the subject. The third is the lens opening. Any photographic light meter will then give you the proper time of exposure. However, in this case, if the exposure required was over five seconds, then a filter to change the color balance needed to be added. Fourth, the filter absorbs some of the light reaching the film, and thus the exposure had to be lengthened to account for the filter. Sixth, after five seconds of exposure, the film reacts to light more slowly (reciprocity) and therefore the exposure has to be lengthened. Seventh, since the netsuke is so small, the lens is a longer than normal distance from the film in order to achieve an attractive size image on the film. This causes the eighth variable, bellows extension. When one of my lenses is used to capture a larger than life-size image of a netsuke on film, the bellows extension causes the normal exposure to be multiplied by 16 times. That would cause the one-second exposure at f/16 mentioned above to take over 16 minutes!

In creating the lighting to photograph these miniature sets, it was important to establish as much overall lighting as possible. Even though the subjects themselves were usually about two inches tall, I used two four-foot by eight-foot translucent panels to soften the light entering the area (a) from the front. An additional panel was set up over

a

the set to create a feeling of natural sunlight. This general set up was then custom tailored for each image.

Nearly every image also required additional lighting to be directed at the netsuke, or parts of the netsuke, to bring out details. A good example is the cover photograph, which required three additional light sources to help illuminate the undercut folds of the costume. These additional lights were created by bouncing light into the area with a mirror and aluminum foil. An additional electric light was also needed. Just adding light was rarely enough to complete the effects that you see. Often, shadows had to be created. They were usually needed in the background to help create a visual separation between the netsuke and the·setting.

One example of the difference that lighting can make is the mask of Shojo, (a) and (b). Which image do you prefer? Can you think of another way to illuminate the mask?

a *b*

When photographing netsuke, the angle of view is critically important. While it is true that the netsuke is carved in full dimension, and that all parts are equally, impeccably finished, there is usually one very precise angle at which the essence of the image is strongest. There usually are several "good" angles of view, and those may even change with the viewer, but there is also usually just one outstanding view. And, of course, this harkens back to the original usage. When the netsuke was "on display" at the top of the *obi*, there was only one basic angle of view. Some artists of the Iwami School took advantage of this and created images carved along one side of a boar's tooth. When you contemplate photographing your netsuke, you must discover what is the precisely best angle.

The cover photograph also illustrates this point. I had photographed the Sambaso dancer in front of a golden screen. The netsuke looked fine, but something was not quite right about the overall photograph. I noticed that the bottom edge of his right sleeve was contiguous with the black border on the screen. By moving the camera just one-half inch lower, a sliver of golden screen glowed under the bottom edge of the kimono sleeve to delineate it and bring some brightness to that section of the image.

Photographing anything this small is a challenge. Just getting room enough around the equipment to let light fall on the subject is a challenge. Every time that you touch something in the scene with size XXL hands, it's a challenge. And speaking of challenges, in case you have never looked into a studio camera before, I thought that you would be interested to see that the image is upside down and backwards!

Photographing netsuke is an exciting experience, in spite of, or maybe even because of the challenges. There is something different about them, as HIH Prince Norihito of Takamado states in the Foreword. They do have a "twist" that sets them apart from mere technical exercises in carving, and from all but the finest of other sculpture. Discovering that special element and then attempting to translate it into a two-dimensional photograph is a special challenge that few photographers can meet.

Netsuke Collecting

Notes on Netsuke Collecting

When it became time to design a cover for this book, I selected two images. I liked each one for different reasons. The first one that I chose is now Plate 4, Little One-Inch. I like the image. I like the story. I think that it portrays the idea of "Japanese life and legend" without even knowing the story.

The second image that I chose was of the Sambaso dancer. It is a powerful netsuke that is a wonderful piece of sculpture, an exquisite example of lacquer painting, and also has a definite "Japanese" quality about the whole image.

I would have chosen Little One-Inch for the cover. The editors chose the Sambaso dancer. Little One-Inch was loaned to me by the couple that has given me great support in producing this book. They loaned many of the netsuke that you see, and also provided access to reference materials that were not in my personal library. I would have enjoyed relating why they chose to collect Little One-Inch.

My wife and I own the little Sambaso dancer. In fact, he is the first netsuke that we acquired. The editors were not aware of this information when they chose him for the cover. It happened that I had done a significant amount of work for Mr. Ralph deVille, owner of the Stone Lantern mentioned previously. I offered to trade out a portion of the work for an unspecified art treasure from his shop. We arrived at the appropriate amount to trade and then I waited for two months before I was again in North Carolina to consummate the transaction.

When we first arrived, Ralph unwrapped a tiny box and presented the netsuke Sambaso dancer before me. I admired it. He put it away. Then Ralph and I did some business things while my wife continued to roam the shop, scouting out things to trade for. After business, I too joined the search. We were trading a significant amount of value for this as yet undiscovered art object. What would it be? The Stone Lantern has grown into several connecting stores, all on different levels, and every possible display place has an Oriental gem or treasure. But what would we choose? We discussed many possibilities over lunch. When we returned to the shop, our decision was made—a large sang-de-boeuf Chinese porcelain vase.

It was on a shelf some nine feet above the floor. As I told Ralph of our decision, and waited for a step ladder to be brought, I happened to ask him what he would have chosen for that value. His answer was clear—the tiny netsuke.

"But," I stammered, "its unsigned."

Ralph simply took the netsuke out of the box, held it up and asked, "Does that matter?"

The answer then, as now, is, "Of course not." He is a wonderful work of art, full of spirit, and the chauffeur for a magic-carpet ride into the land of netsuke that has taken my wife and me halfway around the world and across three centuries in time, learning about the life and legends of Japan.

Many people have enjoyed collecting these fascinating works of art. Most are at first enraptured by the exquisite details and superb carving shown in these tiny figures. Some enjoy "trick" carvings, such as the peach that has a secret compartment that unscrews to reveal a miniscule chain, all carved out of one piece of ivory (Plate 49). Some netsuke have movable parts, such as the jaw that moves on the skull (Plate 61.) However, most collectors are eventually captivated by the pure artistic quality of the netsuke. Signed netsuke account for less than half of the existing pieces, and most early works are unsigned. It was only after 1920 that netsuke carvers began to create netsuke as art objects, rather than primarily functional objects, and to sign their work. Neither age nor a signature is a good criteria for purchasing one, as netsuke by living masters bring prices higher than the majority of antique pieces, and many spurious signatures have been added to mediocre pieces.

If you decide to collect only netsuke by living master carvers, then the general rule about the signature is changed. It is the general practice of contemporary netsuke carvers to sign their works, as do most other contemporary artists. Therefore, the seller should be able to provide you with the name of the artist, the approximate or exact date of creation, and any other information that might interest you.

The rarity of the material out of which they are carved may affect the price, but an inspired netsuke carved out of wood would be more valuable than an awkward piece made from ivory. Prices vary from a few dollars to over one hundred thousand dollars.

Some people collect by specialty type of netsuke such as *sashi* (long narrow ones), *manju* (flat disc-shaped ones), or by materials such as metal, ivory, or ceramics. Others collect by subject.

Whatever the subject, whether it is masks, occupations, nature, monkeys, or any other aspect of Japanese culture, there is a collector who specializes in that field. Another way of collecting is by school of carvers. Some people only collect netsuke that have been handled for generations to develop that charming patina that only comes from use. Others prefer the crispness of a squeaky-clean carving obtained fresh from the contemporary carver's hand.

One of the collectors who loaned me several exquisite pieces for this book, also owns some pieces that are outright copies of famous pieces. They were bought knowing they are copies. Many of the netsuke currently available through flea markets and some "antique shows" are modern copies of antique pieces. If the netsuke that you are coveting costs more than you can comfortably afford, then you should have a reputable dealer check it out, or only buy from a reputable netsuke dealer to begin with.

One way to develop your own knowledge about netsuke is to join the Netsuke Kenkyukai Society. It is a study group that produces a very informative magazine that will help you learn more about all aspects of netsuke.

If you want to make the decision of which netsuke to collect on your own, you may want to use a method that has worked for me. Look at all of the material that is available. Narrow the choice down to your top few favorite pieces. Study each one carefully. Then leave. Go home. Go to lunch, or just take a walk. As soon as you step out of the door, you will begin to think about one of those treasures—even worry that someone might buy it before you get back. If you don't love it enough to worry about it, keep walking, the bug hasn't bit you hard enough, yet. You *may* still escape! However, when you do return, you will know without a doubt which netsuke is best for you.

Whatever your original reason for liking them, netsuke can now be your miniature guide to the life and legends of the Japanese people.

NETSUKE
Japanese Life and Legend in Miniature

Plate 1

Subject: Basket and Gourd
Artist: Masatsugu (Kaigyokusai)
Material: Wood and Split Bamboo
Date: Early nineteenth century
Size: Basket 4 1/2" x 4 1/2" x 2 5/8"
       Gourd 5 3/4" x 1" x 3/4"

Perhaps this is as close to an original style of netsuke as we will find available today. The gourd is elegantly and simply carved out of wood, and the basket is impeccably rendered in a fine weave of split bamboo. This set shows how the netsuke originated—as a utilitarian way of keeping a small carrying case from slipping out from under the belt *(obi)* of the Japanese gentleman's kimono.

Usually, the netsuke would have been slipped up between the *obi* and the kimono, then flopped over the top of the *obi*. The basket would then hang from the cord passing behind the *obi,* leaving the gentleman's hands free. This elongated style is called a *sashi*-netsuke, and was usually inserted from the top of the *obi,* leaving a decorative portion peeking over the edge, and the cord and basket dangling in front of the *obi.*

In the original form, the gourd, which is the netsuke, may have been an actual dried gourd, an attractive root, or a stone with holes in it to facilitate fastening a cord to it. The netsuke was utilitarian in that it was used as a kind of stopper for the end of the cord, but it also gave the user a good deal of pleasure: The person using it chose the object because it looked good, had an attractive surface to it, and held the basket in place.

What we see here as a basket might have been a cloth or leather pouch. As a need for separate compartments became necessary to hold money, medicines, and other items, the *inro* was developed. It is a series of small boxes that are all connected "in a row." The boxes are so impeccably crafted that the lacquer design often painted on the surface is continuous from one to another.

Born Shimizu Tokuo in 1813, Masatsugu, who later adopted the name Kaigyokusai, became one of the greatest netsuke carvers in history. He once destroyed a carving that he had just created of a mushroom basket when some children couldn't recognize the subject.

Plate 2

Subject: Monkey Studying Netsuke and Inro
Artist: Masatami
Material: Ivory
Date: Mid-ninteenth century
Size: 1 ³/₈" x 1 ⁵/₈" x 1 ³/₈"

The monkey is the animal symbol for the ninth year of the Oriental zodiac. In addition to representing a month, each zodiac sign also corresponds to a time of the day. Since the day is twenty-four hours long, it represents a period of two hours' duration. The monkey represents the period between 3 and 5 P.M. in Western time.

To be born in the year of the monkey is fortunate because it is the same year as the birth of Hideyoshi—the "monkey-faced adventurer" who was born in the monkey year and who succeeded in raising himself from a low-born position to that of administrator of the Empire with the title *Taiko*, or Great Prince.

One Japanese proverb refers to a conceited person who annoyingly displays his learning as "a monkey with a hat on." The Japanese language is filled with puns. The netsuke carver often takes a humorous look at society, legends, and folktales. In this netsuke, perhaps he is poking fun at both the creator of the work and the collector.

There are two different artists in this book that used the name Masatami. The earlier Masatami flourished in the mid-nineteenth century (1848-53). He excelled in carving rats and monkeys with intricate details, mostly from ivory. As may be expected from a carver that used the same subject many times, there are numerous variations on a theme.

The second Masatami (1853-1928) was born Moribe Fukuzo, and was active into the early twentieth century. His excellent carvings, in both wood and ivory show the same fascination with realistic attention to detail as the first Masatami.

Plate 3

Subject: Pine Cone
Artist: Keisai
Material: Wood
Date: Mid-nineteenth century
Size: 1 7/8" x 5/8" diameter

In Japan, the pine trees are perhaps more picturesque than in any other country. There are several different kinds, and they are generally named by growth characteristics, such as the white (needle) pine, black (needle) pine, or the brocade (bark) pine. They are treasured as symbols of longevity and therefore are often found in Japanese gardens. Many famous pine trees are over 800 years old.

A very special pine-tree bonsai was donated to the people of the United States by the people of Japan to celebrate the bicentennial of America. It was one of a group of 50 bonsai that were donated by Japanese citizens. They are now on display daily in a special pavilion at the U.S. National Arboretum in Washington, D.C.

The oldest tree donated is a Japanese white pine. It is a special cultivar called *Miyajima.* It has short, straight, silver-green needles, which give it the illusion of being a large tree even when it is quite small. This type of pine does not reproduce naturally in the wild. It is a special type that must be propagated by making cuttings or layerings from the parent plant. This particular tree was created by a Japanese gardener over 350 years ago—a century and a half before the American revolution! It grew healthy and strong under the loving care of succeeding generations of Japanese gardeners for over 350 years, and is now being cared for by American bonsai masters.

A very special technique is used to shape pine trees, whether they are growing in a garden or in a container. In late spring a portion of each new sprout is picked off. Some are eliminated all together, while others are encouraged to grow. Wires, strings, and weights are often used to shape a branch's growth. One tree in the garden of the Golden Pavilion in Kyoto has been in training for 300 years to attain the shape of a sailboat.

A netsuke such as this one of a pine cone and two small needles can serve to remind the viewer of their own favorite pine tree, wherever that may be, any place in the world.

Keisai, born Matsushita Kiichiro, was a pupil of the great master Kyusai (Plate 63).

Plate 4

Subject: Little One-Inch
Artist: Gyokusho
Material: Ivory
Date: ca. 1952
Size: 1 3/4" x 1 1/2" x 1 1/4"

A married couple had tried for years to have children, but had been unsuccessful. They traveled to a shrine and offered prayers asking for a child. On their way home they heard a tiny crying sound coming from a clump of grass. In the grass, they found a tiny baby boy. They realized that this was the answer to their prayers, and they took the little boy home. They raised him as their own son, even though he was only about the size of a thumb.

Years went by, and the boy grew no taller. By then, everyone was calling him "Little One-Inch." One day, although he was still only one inch tall, he decided that he was old enough to leave home and seek his fortune. His parents would miss him, but they helped him prepare for the journey. They gave him a rice bowl for a boat, a chopstick for an oar, and a needle for a sword.

After he had floated on the river for many miles, a frog accidentally bumped into his boat and spilled him into the water. When he swam to the shore, he was at the home of a wealthy lord. The lord liked the little boy, and let him stay, becoming a playmate for his daughter, the princess. They would play together all of the time, and sometimes, as in this netsuke, he would take a nap right on her wooden sandal.

One day he and the princess were on their way to visit a temple when a giant ogre appeared. He tried to catch the princess. Little One-Inch drew his sword and stabbed the ogre in the foot. But ogre skin is very tough, so he did not even feel it. As he climbed up the ogre to brandish his sword at the ogre's nose, he saw a magic hammer that the ogre possessed. He jumped into the ogre's mouth and started poking the giant green tongue with his needle-sword. This really hurt the ogre who spit Little One-Inch out onto the ground. As the ogre was running away, he dropped his magic hammer.

The princess quickly ran over and picked up the hammer. Shaking it she cried, "Please let Little One-Inch grow taller." With each shake of the hammer, he grew an inch taller. She shook and shook and shook the hammer until they were exactly the same height.

Everyone was very happy with what had happened, and when they were both a little older, the lord blessed their marriage and they lived a long and happy life together.

Born Toshio Suzuki in 1926, Gyokusho, who studied under Gyokudo, is well known for the delicate, finely executed netsuke that have a warmth of human feeling.

Plate 5

Subject: Tiger and Cub
Artist: Kangyoku
Material: Mammoth ivory
Date: Early 1990
Size: 2" x 1 7/8" x 1 3/8"

Like the lion, the tiger is a stranger to the Japanese islands, and was usually portrayed in the traditional manner imported from China via scroll paintings. It was long assumed to be a mythical beast and is the symbol of courage. It is said to live a thousand years. When it reaches the age of five hundred, a character meaning "king" is said to appear on its head, and at the age of a thousand, it becomes an inhabitant of the Milky Way.

The tiger is the animal symbol for the third year of the Japanese zodiac. In Oriental symbology, there has long been a conventional connection between the tiger and bamboo. The tiger is often shown forcing its way through the thick undergrowth of the jungle, thus symbolizing "Will" overcoming "Evil." When a tiger is shown crouching beside a clump of bamboo in a storm, the tiger is a symbol of the power of faith. And it takes quite a lot of faith for the Japanese to believe in the images of tigers, since tigers are not native to Japan. On the other hand, there are many creatures in Japanese legends that are only visible in paintings or sculpture—*kirin,* dragons, *kappa,* and *oni* being just a few.

The current Kangyoku (III), born in 1944, learned carving from his father, Kangyoku II, a descendant of the great nineteenth-century carver, Hojitsu (d. 1892), and a popular *okimono* carver in the Tokyo area. His carving specialty is animals, as can be seen from this contemporary tiger and cub as well as the Japanese badger (Plate 10) and long-toed mouse (Plate 31) that he carved nearly twenty years ago. His work has a freshness to it, a contemporary flair, as well as a traditional compactness of form and quality of carving. In the late 1970s, he changed his carving style and began adding *"Risshisai"* to his signature to mark this new stage of his career. *Risshisai* means "striving to be the best."

Through his work and that of many of the other fine contemporary carvers, the art of netsuke has been revived. Although netsuke are not commonly worn today, they are highly sought after by collectors of fine art.

Plate 6

Subject: Spider, Fly on Lotus Leaf
Artist: Iwami school
Material: Wood
Date: Nineteenth century
Size: 2 1/8" x 1 7/8" x 7/8"

Two full moons had faded since the lotus was in full bloom, pushing its huge flower above the bold round leaves at the edge of the pond. The cicada's call still filled the air to accompany the petal's dance across bobbing leaves, skipping, dropping, falling to the still wet shore.

A leaf, probably among the first to emerge in the rush of spring growth, also let leave of the upright stem and its place in the now shortening sunshine hours. Once a brilliant green foil to the blossom's pure whiteness, it splashed heavily into the stagnant water below.

Gliding on the crimson waves of autumn, the spent umbrella of youth traveled to another shore. Folded by time and wind, it found safe haven among the slick stones and became the background for a different play. A night spent warily perched on the rolled lotus lookout point gave solace to the summer-weary fly. Drifting crimson maple leaves foretold of bitter dampness, snow, and ice. Not the menu of choice for a summer fly.

Contemplating spinning the last web of fall to ensure a full winter's larder, the spider awoke under the lotus leaf, stretched one leg and then another and then another and then another,... and, moving with the slowness of January molasses, pulled itself onto the lotus stage. The heavy winter like cold kept it from moving faster. Attention, accelerating in the rush of the hunt, focused now on the rim of the pad: a lump, a bump, a fly!

Web unspun, undauntedly creeping slowly forward until the delicate morsel was barely out of reach, the spider paused, body still akimbo to wonder which the morning sun would warm faster, fly wings or spider legs.

As the netsuke carver sits alone in his studio, perhaps these are the kinds of thoughts that filter through his fertile mind as he spends hours, days, and weeks, working on a single fine quality netsuke.

Plate 7

Subject: Demon Catcher and Two Demons
Artist: Minkoku
Material: Wood and Ivory
Date: Late eighteenth century
Size: 1 1/4" x 1 5/8" x 1 1/8"

Shoki, a giant spiritual figure, was the protector of Emperor Genso (713–55). He once saved the Emperor from a fatal disease and on another occasion appeared in the night to drive away an intruder attempting to steal the Empresses' belongings. His spirit continues to search out and expel demons *(oni),* wherever they may be. In many instances, the demons that he is catching are playing impish tricks on him, even getting him to hide under his own hat, while the demon or *oni* sits on top of it. In this example, he has caught two *oni.* One of them is playing with the thunder drum.

Oni is the generic name given to all evil spirits. Usually, they are small, humanlike creatures with horns on their heads. They often wear only a loincloth, usually made of tiger skin. They have a fierce appearance, with a large mouth filled with tusks. *Oni* are, however, able to attain salvation by doing such good deeds as working in temples.

In olden days, the passing of the old year was celebrated on Setsubun, the eve of the first day of spring. It is now celebrated on the third or fourth of February. On this day, it is customary to exorcise evil spirits. Toward dusk, dried, roasted soybeans are scattered inside and outside the house to the chant of "Out with demons! In with good luck!"

Therefore, *oni* are often shown hiding under a box or basket to escape from the soybeans. The ceremony is still done today in some areas, even by families living in the midst of modern Tokyo.

Minkoku (fl. 1789–1800) excelled at carving figural netsuke. His superb technique brought him great fame during his lifetime. It is thought that he was a direct student of Shugetsu I.

Plate 8

Subject: Cat with a Ladybug on Tail
Artist: Kenji
Material: Ivory
Date: Late twentieth century
Size: 1 3/4" x 1 3/4" x 1 1/2"

There are native wild cats in Japan as well as pet cats. The Japanese cat has a naturally bobbed tail. One popular ukiyo-e calendar of the nineteenth century featured charming images of Japanese cats at play. The same subject is popular today in large-format color photographs.

In the latter part of the twentieth century, other breeds of cats began to be imported to Japan, and today, Persians, Siamese, and others are very popular.

As we might expect, there are many "cat sayings." Here are a few:

> *The cat forgets in three days, the kindness that it has received*
> *for three years.*
> *Even three inches above the ground, the cat can turn a somersault.*
> *The cat shuts its eyes while it steals the cream.*
> *Don't set a cat to protect a dried fish.*

This charming Persian cat has been rudely aroused from a peaceful afternoon nap by a ladybug's landing on its tail. This is a very interesting subject for a netsuke because it combines certain qualities found in the finest traditional pieces with a bold new insight.

This is the work of Kenji Abe (b. 1947), the son of the well known contemporary carver, Godo Abe (b. 1914), who is still actively carving. Kenji studied under Toshikatsu Kobari as well as under his father.

Plate 9

Subject: Ginkgo Nuts
Artist: Unsigned
Material: Ivory
Date: ca. 1900
Size: 1" x 1 7/8" x 1 1/16"

The ginkgo *(Ginkgo biloba)* is a deciduous forest tree that evolved during the last botanical period. It is native only to China and Japan. However, since it is very resistant to air pollution, it is being planted in many cities around the world. It grows to be 40 feet tall and can measure 30 feet in circumference. The fan-shaped leaves have parallel veins that somewhat resemble the webbed foot of a duck. In Japan, it is often referred to as *icho,* which is a pun on the two Chinese characters that mean "duck foot."

There are many famous old ginkgo trees that have been designated as "National Treasures" by the Japanese government. Most of them are growing in temple grounds. Several Japanese family crests utilize the beautiful simplicity of the ginkgo-leaf design. The ginkgo nut, called *ginnan* (or "silver prune") in Japan, is used in Japanese gourmet cooking.

It is said that another useful quality of the ginkgo nut is that of revealing the slightest amount of poison present in food or drink by emitting a quiet crackling sound.

This netsuke is more than a mere representation of the ginkgo nut, however. It is a powerful sculpture that beautifully balances forms, voids, and line.

The traditional netsuke in the cover illustration, this modern sculptural masterwork, and many other netsuke are not signed. This is *not* an indication of lesser quality, or that it was produced in some Japanese or other workshop. Indeed, just the opposite may be true. Work that was commissioned for the ruling households was rarely signed, as it would be an affront to the ruler to put an artist's or craftsman's name in front of the ruler. Clever carvers throughout the ages have affixed spurious signatures to their own work to increase the marketability of their own product.

Plate 10

Subject: *Tanuki* (Japanese Badger)
Artist: Kangyoku
Material: Ivory
Date: Early 1970s
Size: 1 7/8" x 1 1/8" x 7/8"

The badger *(tanuki),* or raccoon dog, is a real animal that is credited with supernatural powers, as are the fox and the cat. It is a mischievous animal that uses many disguises to deceive and annoy passers-by. Here, he has covered himself with lotus leaves, the sacred emblem of Buddhism, to disguise himself as a Buddhist priest. In this disguise, he begs for religious contributions.

In one *tanuki* story, an old female badger who lived in a cave was worried because her mate had not returned, so she took on a human guise and went into town to find out what had happened to him. There she met the hunter who had slain her mate. The female badger then lectured him on the sin of destroying life. She told him about a man who hunted animals for their skins so that drums could be made of them. When the souls of all the animals he had killed caught up with him, he was sent to hell. There, he learned the doctrines of Buddhism, which include not taking another's life: he then became penitent and offered his own skin to Buddha to make into a drum. The hunter, upon hearing this story, abandoned his former profession forever.

The badger, although filled with regret that her mate was dead, was relieved that she herself would no longer be in danger of being killed by this hunter. She eventually rewarded the hunter for changing his ways by appearing in her true form and performing the belly-drum song or *"Tanuki no hara-tsuzumi."* This is a very special reward that is not seen or heard by many people. Although this *tanuki* tale ends well, in most folktales the *tanuki* is responsible for causing most of the trouble suffered by mankind.

The real *tanuki* is a small animal, brownish in color, having a snout like a fox and a short tail. In his folklore portraits, which include netsuke as well as paintings and sculptures, he is shown in two principal forms. In one he looks like a little bear. In this bear-form he has an enormous belly. Statues of this stylized *tanuki,* usually wearing a hat, are often seen outside the doors of drinking places, enticing customers to come in. In his other form, he looks more like a fox.

Compare this netsuke carved in the early stages of Kangyoku's career with the Tiger and Cub (Plate 5) carved in 1990. You can see that his style has changed significantly and his technique has become very refined, yet he has retained the inspirational warmth and a touch of humor in each of his superb netsuke.

Plate 11

Subject: Crab on a Fishing Trap
Artist: Unsigned
Material: Boxwood
Date: Nineteenth century
Size: 1 1/4" x 1 5/8" x 3/4"

In Western cultures a "crab" is usually an anti-social person and a monkey is usually thought of as gregarious. In this Japanese folktale, the roles are reversed.

A crab and a monkey went for a walk together. They were both lucky and found something. The crab found a rice ball and the monkey found a persimmon seed. The monkey liked to eat rice balls so he talked the crab into letting him trade the rice ball for the persimmon seed. The monkey immediately ate the rice ball. The crab couldn't eat the persimmon seed, even with his strong claws. So he took it home and planted it in the ground. He nourished it and it grew into a fine tree that bore many beautiful persimmons. No matter how hard he tried, the crab couldn't climb the tree to get the ripe fruit, so he asked the monkey to help him.

When the monkey got up in the tree and saw all those beautiful, ripe persimmons, he realized that they were even more delicious than the rice balls. He started to eat them. The crab protested, and asked him to toss some down. The monkey grabbed a hard green one and tossed it at the crab. It hit the crab and hurt him, so he went back home. The monkey kept eating the fruit until they were all gone.

The crab decided to teach the monkey a lesson and asked three of his friends for help. When the monkey came to dinner, the friends were all in hiding. A chestnut was hiding in the coals of the fireplace. When he got very warm, he burst out of the fireplace and burned the monkey on his neck. Just then, the second friend, a hornet, flew in and stung the monkey on his nose. As the monkey got up to run out of the house, the third friend, a mortar, fell on the monkey's head from above the door.

Realizing that he had been outwitted, the monkey bowed down and apologized for eating all of the ripe persimmons and throwing a green one at Mr. Crab. He then asked for forgiveness. Mr. Crab accepted, and they all became good friends again.

Plate 12

Subject: Bamboo Shoot with Frog
Artist: Unsigned
Material: Boxwood
Date: Nineteenth century
Size: 2 9/16" x 2 3/4" x 15/16"

No other country has as large a variety of bamboo as does Japan. Although it is a grass, it is evergreen and thus a symbol of constancy and devotion. It is a lucky plant, especially when combined with the pine and plum; together the three are known as the "three gentlemen." These three plants are always displayed in flower arrangements to be used as New Year's decorations, to symbolize good luck in the coming year.

The Japanese are known for their exceptional feats in the art of archery, or *kyudo.* Japanese archery equipment is elegant and made from all natural materials. The seven-foot-long bows are made from laminated bamboo, and the arrows are made from a different type of bamboo that grows in long, straight, thin culms.

Edison, in first producing an electric lamp, used bamboo filaments obtained from a town between Kyoto and Osaka.

Bamboo is a tree-grass. The biggest specimens come from Java and India, where giant bamboo has been known to reach a height of 120 feet. Bamboo has the most rapid rate of growth of any plant, setting a record of 91 centimeters (or nearly 36 inches) in 24 hours! Some species contain so much silica in the plant cells that they will give off sparks when struck by a piece of steel. Its pulp is used to make fine quality paper. Bamboo shoots are a delicacy, fresh, pickled, or canned.

Bamboo flowers only rarely, and afterwards, the majority of the stand dies back.

A bamboo forest is considered a safe ground in an earthquake, due to the extensive array of densely matted roots that make it nearly impossible for the earth to break apart.

This netsuke definitely shows a frog with its smooth skin as compared to the toads seen in many other netsuke. In this case, the frog's smooth skin was used to emphasize the intricately carved details of the tender young bamboo shoots.

Plate 13

Subject: Monkey
Artist: Ikkan
Material: Wood
Date: Early nineteenth century
Size: 1 5/8" x 1 3/8" x 7/8"

The monkey is the animal symbol for the ninth year of the Oriental zodiac. Marriage in the monkey year is an unlucky omen, because the word for monkey (*saru*) is pronounced the same as the verb "to leave."

The Western cat-and-dog relationship is the same as that between the Japanese monkey and dog. They are often shown in fights, whether the images are realistic or cartoons. In another East-West analogy linking the monkey and the dog, there is a story about some monkeys that try to steal the moon from a well. They see the brilliant reflection of the moon in the well and form a long chain of monkeys to try to catch it. When the branch that they are hanging from breaks, they all fall into the well and drown. The parable is similar to the Aesop fable of the dog dropping the bone from his mouth to try to catch the reflection of the same bone in the river.

The carving of three monkeys at the Toshogu Shrine in Nikko is world-famous. It is called the carving of the "monkeys of the three countries" and is said to represent India, China, and Japan. They also represent another Japanese pun. The word for monkey is *saru,* and the suffix-*zaru* is a negative ending for a verb. Therefore, the three monkeys become symbols for the words *mi-zaru* (seeing not), *kika-zaru* (hearing not), and *iwa-zaru* (speaking not). The English-language translation is, of course, the moralization—"See no evil, hear no evil, speak no evil."

The netsuke carver from Nagoya, Ikkan has been greatly admired for over a century. His talents have been described as "divinely inspired skill." His realistic treatment is derived through his drawings from nature. Rats, dragons, monkeys and sleeping *shojo* (a mythical creature renowned for its fondness for sake) are among his favorite subjects.

Plate 14

Subject: Tiger and Cub
Artist: Okakoto
Material: Ivory
Date: ca. 1835
Size: 1 1/8" x 1 9/16" x 1 1/4"

Since the tiger is a powerful animal, it is the subject of many proverbs and folk sayings. Here are two interesting Japanese "tiger" sayings.

If you keep the tiger from the front gate, there is a wolf at the back gate is the Japanese version of "out of the frying pan, into the fire."

Feeding a tiger, trouble afterwards warns that you cannot change one's basic nature. The tiger will not always be content with your handouts.

The following two sayings seem particularly appropriate for this bold, yet charming netsuke.

If you do not enter the tiger's den, you cannot get her cub tells us "nothing ventured, nothing gained."

One should cherish like a tiger's cub means that something is "the apple of your eye" and by extension, that nothing should dissuade you from defending your family and your ideas.

Images of tigers are sometimes painted on the gates of homes and temples as a symbol of bravery. On the doors of authorities, they are drawn to produce a feeling of awe and terror in all who approach.

The carver Okakoto (fl. 1830–43) specialized in carving animals. He lived mostly in Kyoto, where he was a student of Okatomo. There is one netsuke that was carved on a special occasion and signed, "Okakoto, 80 years old."

Plate 15

Subject: Mountain Deity *(Tengu)*
Artist: Shugetsu
Material: Boxwood
Date: Early nineteenth century
Size: 1 1/4" x 1 1/2" x 1 1/4"

Tengu are deities of the mountains and forest who have supernatural strength and who fiercely protect the solitude and tranquility of their habitat. Hunters, woodcutters, and other people that reside in the mountains particularly venerate the *tengu* and their strength.

There are two types of *tengu*—a small, winged, crow-beaked variety and a tall, humanlike one with an elongated nose. The humanlike ones are protected by the crow *tengu*, portrayed in this netsuke, which are smaller beings with bodies like a person, but with two wings, which enable them to fly. Their nails are like tiger's claws and their eyes are round, exuding light like a lightning bolt. They have beaks like a bird instead of a mouth and they are often shown armed with clubs.

The crow *tengu* is part bird and part human. In the legend of Kintaro, this child of the mountains amused himself by raiding *tengu* nests. He grew to great strength from wrestling with all of the creatures of the mountains, including the *tengu*. An image of Kintaro carrying an enormous axe is often painted on children's kites to inspire them to build great strength in their bodies.

Tengu sometimes take the shape of mountain priests *(yamabushi)*. They then gather in mountain clearings, eat special mushrooms, and carry on throughout the night.

The historical hero, Minamoto no Yoshitsune, is said to have learned prodigious sword-fighting skills from a *tengu* on the top of Mount Kurama in Kyoto while still a young child. Yoshitsune was one of the most famous swordsmen and greatest generals of old Japan. He lived in the twelfth century, but his exploits have survived the centuries in many stories and books.

Shugetsu I was active from 1764-71. He had enjoyed a successful career in painting before turning to carving netsuke. He lived most of his life in Osaka, but spent several years in Tokyo, carving netsuke and *hina* dolls. It was during this period that a 13-year-old youth wandered into his shop and became fascinated, watching him carve. He became an apprentice. Soon the teenager was so skilled that the master allowed him to use the name Shugetsu II. Two other Shugetsu's followed. This *tengu* is probably by Shugetsu II.

Plate 16

Subject: Octopus
Artist: Unsigned
Material: Ivory
Date: Mid-twentieth century
Size: 7/8" x 1 15/16" diameter

All sea creatures lived happily in the palace of the Dragon King deep at the bottom of the sea. The palace doctor was the octopus. For some reason, though, he just did not like the jellyfish. Back then, even the jellyfish had bones and could swim very fast. When the Dragon King's daughter got sick, the octopus doctor recommended that a monkey's liver would cure the daughter. So the King sent the fast jellyfish to get one. The jellyfish happened to find a drowning monkey, and was bringing him back to the King, when the monkey said, "I left my liver hanging on a pine tree on that island over there."

When the jellyfish took him to the tree, the monkey jumped onto the land and ran away. The jellyfish returned to the King and told him this story. All of the other creatures beat him very badly for not bringing back the monkey's liver to save the King's daughter. In fact, they broke every one of his bones. When the octopus saw this happening, he just laughed and laughed.

Just then the Princess came running in and told everyone that she was not sick after all, it had just been a tummy-ache. The wise Dragon King knew that the octopus had recognized the stomachache from the beginning and had done all of this just to hurt the jellyfish. He felt very sorry for the jellyfish and angry at the octopus.

The jellyfish became the favorite creature of the Dragon King, and, even though he has no bones, and swims ever so slowly now, he is never bothered by any of the other creatures of the sea. To punish him for the terrible experience that he had caused the jellyfish, the Dragon King banished the octopus from his palace forever. And that is why the octopus always lives alone.

Plate 17

Subject: Mushrooms and Spider
Artist: Attributed to Ganbun
Material: Wood and Silver
Date: ca. 1890
Size: 1 5/8" x 1 3/8" x 5/8"

Mushrooms and other fungi are often subjects of netsuke. Most of the time, however, the mushrooms are depicted in groups of whole mushrooms as though they were growing in a field. The mushroom thus illustrated is a symbol of maleness, just as the peach is the vegetative symbol of femaleness.

Just as the American Indians knew of the power of certain types of mushrooms, so did the Japanese mountain priests called *yamabushi*.

There are many types of edible mushrooms found in Japan. In this netsuke, the mushroom stems have been removed and the caps have been piled up, ready to be taken home. Perhaps they have been left sitting there a little too long because some insects have eaten holes in them—and there is even a spider on one of them now!

In Western art traditions, there is a history of master painters and sculptors hiring assistants or apprentices to assist in the various stages required to bring a work of art from raw materials to completion. This is the same concept as the traditional Japanese apprentice system, in which beginning students will do only the most fundamental work for years. Progress in refinement only comes as their skills warrant. However, there is an Eastern tradition that is rarely found in the West—two or more masters collaborating in creating a single work of art.

There are many examples of several master painters celebrating a particularly enjoyable party by collaborating on a single work. One may do the rocks, another orchids, another bamboo, etc. Many netsuke that combine materials, such as this one, were collaborations of two artists. However, the mid-Meiji-era netsuke artist Ganbun was skilled at both wood carving and metalwork. The metal spider is made from a silver/copper alloy called *shibuichi* that is a subdued grayish silver when new. It eventually tarnishes to a jet black. Ganbun often used this material to fashion ants, which he then applied to other nature subjects.

Plate 18

Subject: Bird Vendor
Artist: Kunimitsu
Material: Ivory
Date: 1970s
Size: 2" x 1 1/4" x 1 1/4"

This netsuke shows a bird vendor checking his merchandise—a cage with two small birds in it. The incredible skill required to carve out a bird cage is beyond the comprehension of we mere mortals. Yet there are also two birds within the cage—all carved from a single piece of ivory!

The Japanese tradesman is proud of his wares. Even today, merchandise is proudly displayed in front of many shops. These displays are of fine merchandise, and are cared for each day. Even today, at the start of each business day, you can see shop owners sweep the sidewalk in front of their own shops. Later, they bring out water to physically wash it clean and symbolically purify the area of evil influences.

Likewise, the bird vendor attends to his wares daily—not only to make sure that the birds are healthy, but also because of the pride he takes in his business.

The contemporary carver, Kunimitsu, who was active until 1984, specialized in portraying tradesmen. There are many examples of his work (*see also* Plates 33 and 65). One of the interesting aspects is that, although he utilized the traditional style of hair and clothes, you can see that each carving is a portrait of the artist.

Plate 19

Subject: Sparrow
Artist: Unsigned
Material: Ivory
Date: Nineteenth century
Size: 1 15/16" x 1 15/16" x 3/4"

The sparrow signifies friendship and hard work. A popular children's toy shows the sparrow puffed up and with its wings spread as in this netsuke.

One folktale tells about a man who wanted to give his overlord a special present, and sent to China for a number of sparrows. When one of them died during the trip home, a Japanese sparrow was added. The overlord was impressed by the magnificent gift, but wondered why there was one Japanese sparrow among the Chinese birds. His vassal answered: "As they are all foreigners, they needed an interpreter."

Japanese popular tales usually have a moral and often start with some type of terrible thing happening to one of the main characters. Even though they have been poorly treated by an opponent, they remain generous to their friends. One such tale is that of the cut-tongue sparrow.

An old man had a pet sparrow that he took very good care of; however, one day it was missing. When he asked his neighbor about the sparrow, she said that it had hopped into her yard and eaten some of the paste she was about to use to starch her linen. So she caught it and, to teach it a lesson, cut out its tongue. The sparrow then flew away.

The old man was very upset, so he went into the woods looking for his pet. At last, he found the pet sparrow. The sparrow invited the old man to his own home. After a delightful visit, the sparrow offered the old man a choice of two presents, a large one and a small one. The old man chose the small one, because it would be easier to carry.

When he got back home, he opened the small box and found that it was filled with an unending supply of silver, gold, and jewels. The wicked neighbor saw this and immediately went out into the forest to search for the sparrow.

When they met, the sparrow invited her to his home. When she was ready to leave, he offered her a similar choice of two gifts. She chose the large gift, even though she could hardly lift it. She struggled to carry it home, but became so tired that she had to put it down to rest. When she eagerly looked into the basket, thousands of goblins and devils jumped out and attacked her. The old man eventually adopted a son, and they both lived happily all of their days.

Plate 20

Subject: Boar
Artist: Unsigned
Material: Wood
Date: Twentieth century
Size: 1 1/8" x 1 3/8" x 3/4"

The Japanese zodiac concludes with a dynamic animal, the wild boar. It is particularly admired for its fortitude, perseverance, and reckless courage. Boars rarely retreat, and never stop once they charge.

Nitta Shiro Tadatsune was a general during the early Kamakura period. In May of 1193, he accompanied Shogun Yoritomo on a hunting expedition at the base of Mount Fuji. A huge boar attacked the party with great ferocity. Shiro leaped on its back, killing it with his knife while it was still running. This event has been immortalized in many paintings, ukiyo-e and in some netsuke.

The boar received a Japanese nickname in a rather odd way. When Buddhism was introduced into Japan, many Japanese adopted it as their religion. One of the results of this was that they could no longer eat red meat. This would have caused a problem for both the butchers and their customers, who cherished being able to eat something other than fish in an island country. The nickname *yama kujira* ("mountain whale") appeased the Buddhist law, even though, in fact, whales are warm-blooded mammals, also.

In 1990, a Japanese wild boar became famous by being on international television. If baseball is the American national sport, perhaps Pachinko is the Japanese national pastime. This vertical pinball machine is ubiquitous in Japan. Even so, it was newsworthy when a Pachinko parlor in Takanabe in Miyazaki Prefecture, on the island of Kyushu was visited by a wild boar. It just wandered in through an open door. However, when it discovered that it needed actual money to play the machines, it decided to leave. (Or it may have been because the manager of the Pachinko parlor was chasing it with a stick and a hammer.) When the 50-kilo (or 110-pound) boar found the plate glass front door closed, it never even slowed down. In the greatest of wild boar traditions, he charged straight through it.

Plate 21

Subject: Snake, Toad, and Hoe
Artist: Masatami
Material: Boxwood
Date: Early twentieth century
Size: 5 1/2" x 1 3/4" x 1"

The sign for the sixth year of the Japanese zodiac is the snake. The time of the snake is from 9 to 11 A.M. The snake is also in the retinue of the Japanese Venus—Benten—the goddess of music and the arts. One of the Seven Gods of Good Fortune, she is often represented with a snake coiled around the rock on which she is seated playing a lute. Benten is the only female among the Seven Gods of Good Fortune.

The snake appears in many Japanese proverbs—*use a snake to catch a snake*, or "it takes one to know one"; *poke a bush and drive out a snake*, or "let sleeping dogs lie"; *a blind man is not afraid of a snake*, or "ignorance is bliss"; and *the man who has once been bitten by the snake fears every piece of rope*, or "once bitten, twice shy."

In viewing this netsuke, we must marvel at the skill of the carver, who has contrasted the rigid handle of the hoe with the writhing, sinuous character of the snake. The combination is a tour-de-force in carving that could easily be enjoyed for those attributes alone. Yet, there is a small toad on the blade of the hoe. Is there another level of meaning, of enjoyment to this piece?

There are several stories which center upon three animals—the toad, the snail, and the snake. This triplet is called *"San-sukumi"* or the three who are afraid of each other. Why? The snake can eat the toad, which can eat the snail, but the snail's slimy secretion is fatal to the snake when he digests the toad.

Is this toad sitting on the hoe searching for something to eat, or has he already eaten a snail? The question then becomes a serious one, similar to the ending of the well-known story *The Lady or the Tiger*. Perhaps that is why the snake itself forms a giant question mark.

This tour-de-force in wood carving is by the second Masatami who lived in Nagoya from 1853 to 1928. He was a pupil of Masakazu.

Plate 22

Subject: Tiger in Thick Bamboo
Artist: Tametaka School
Material: Boxwood
Date: Mid-nineteenth century
Size: 1 5/8" x 1 1/4" x 1 1/4"

In many representations, the tiger is associated with bamboo. This seems quite natural, since the bamboo forest is the tiger's lair. However, Oriental philosophers see various meanings in the association.

Even the tiger, the strongest terrestrial animal, needs the assistance of the weak bamboo against the elements. Treading his way through the hostile jungle, he represents the power of good over evil. The protection given the tiger by the bamboo symbolizes the homage of the weak to the strong. Toy tigers are often given to youngsters as an expression of the hope that they will be as strong and courageous as tigers.

Bamboo is the most important Japanese plant. It is used to build their homes, to make many things of daily life, as material for works of art, and as food (the young shoots). The bamboo is the symbol of long life, steadfastness, and fidelity.

As a zodiac sign, the tiger is third in the order of rotation. When applied to time, it represents the period between 3 and 5 A.M.

The artist Tametaka (fl. 1781–88) lived in Nagoya and specialized in carving wooden netsuke. He is said to have originated the technique of carving raised designs. He was though of as an eccentric, yet he established a school of carvers, from which this piece is attributed.

Plate 23

Subject: Toad on a Well Bucket
Artist: Unsigned
Material: Boxwood
Date: Mid-nineteenth century
Size: 1 3/8" x 1 1/4" x 1 1/16"

According to one old tale, the toad lives in the moon. Although there are many stories about toads, this netsuke seems to be the carver's delightful excursion into rendering natural textures. The well-bucket is old, showing every line of the weathered grain of the wood. Some areas are even worn through. In fact, this well bucket has been discarded.

The ritual water basin behind it is a natural rock that has a water-holding area in the top of it. A bamboo ladle is laying there to dip water from the basin. Before entering any temple or shrine in Japan, visitors pour water over their hands as a symbolic cleansing. The water is delivered to this catch basin through a water spout made of natural materials so that it will harmonize with the rest of the garden. The dark stone is a stepping stone so that a person can reach the water basin without getting wet.

The use of water, water basins, and the purifying power of water are very important to the Japanese. Most gardens have some source of water in them—even if it is an imaginary waterway formed by dry gravel raked into water patterns.

As in the West, there are questions such as "How long will it take for a frog to get out of a well if he jumps half the distance to the top each day?" In this netsuke, the answer is, "Until he jumps onto the well-bucket and is pulled out with it."

Plate 24

Subject: Sandal Maker
Artist: Rokugo
Material: Boxwood
Date: Early nineteenth century
Size: 1 3/4" x 1 1/4" x 1 3/8"

This sandal maker is in a working position characteristic of the thousands of different traditional Japanese craftsmen that produce daily goods. Since there are no chairs in a traditional Japanese house, everyone is used to sitting on the floor. Sometimes they may kneel or squat, but for any length of time, they sit on the floor directly or on a pillow. Even contemporary master netsuke carvers such as Bishu carry on this tradition.

The sitting posture gives a solid base. Often the legs, knees, and even toes are used in production of the item. In traditional Japanese bow-making, the feet are used to steady the bow while wedges are driven into a rope that has been wound around the bow. The wedges help shape the bow and provide clamping pressure for the glue that binds the bamboo laminates together.

Here, the sandal maker has fastened the beginning of the braid to his toe to keep the proper amount of tension on the weaving.

Plate 25

Subject: Goddess of Mercy in a Lotus-leaf Boat
Artist: Meido
Material: Ivory
Date: Early twentieth century
Size: 1 5/8" x 1 7/8" x 1 1/8"

The Japanese version of the Goddess of Mercy, Kannon, is perhaps the most elegant of her many manifestations. She had seen many lands and customs before arriving in Japan. Arabian camel-drivers, centuries before Buddha was born, carried an image of "the god who harkens." At that time, it was a male god. He was adopted by followers in Ceylon and in India where he was known as Avalokiteshvara.

When his worship was adopted by the Chinese, characters were chosen for the name that mean "Regarder of the Cries of the World." Even though the figure was originally male, when the Chinese and Japanese adopted this deity, they made it into the Goddess of Mercy known as Kuan-yin (in China) or Kannon (in Japan). She is the goddess of infinite compassion and manifests herself in many different ways. Sometimes she is shown with a carp, another image is of her seated on a rock near a waterfall. A familiar porcelain figure shows her holding a single lotus blossom. She is often shown holding a scroll that contains petitions for assistance from her followers as seen in this netsuke.

In one representation, she is shown as having "a thousand hands." The image represents her merciful desire to reach out to help all peoples. In this form, she is usually rendered with multiple arms arrayed around her as though emanating from her shoulder-blades. The hand for each arm is shown holding a Buddhistic emblem. In Kyoto, the Sanjusangen-do temple contains thirty-three thousand images of this Kannon. There are one thousand gilded statues, each five feet high. They are arranged in tiers, all in one room, over one hundred yards long. These one thousand statues flank a large gilded statue of the seated Kannon. The thirty-three thousand images include the images of Kannon in halos, headdresses, and in the hands of the larger statues.

The temple was established in 1132 but was destroyed by fire. It has been re-built, and you can visit it today and see the thirty-three thousand Kannons as they were restored in 1266.

The temple is also the site of an annual *kyudo* (Japanese archery) competition established in 1606 (*See also* Plate 59).

An expert carver of ivory, specializing in both netsuke and *okimono,* Meido was asked by the Ministry of Agriculture and Commerce to exhibit some of his works at the Great Columbian Exposition in the United States in 1893.

Plate 26

Subject: Demon with Tail Caught in Clam Shell
Artist: Gyokuzan
Material: Yellow Sandalwood
Date: Early nineteenth century
Size: 1 7/8" x 1 3/4" x 1 1/4"

How exasperating! An *oni*, one of the little demons that are so clever that they are always playing tricks on people and even Shoki, the demon catcher, has been trapped himself. Was he caught by a creature much more clever than himself? No! His tail is stuck in a clam shell.

This little scene serves to remind us that every culture has its own ways of telling us to be careful not to get caught up in our own day-to-day affairs.

Some Japanese folktales are told in the style of today's popular horror stories. Or perhaps, Stephen King and other such authors are telling stories in a traditional Japanese style. Here is an example about a terrible demon that did not get away.

Once there was a terrible female demon—an ogress—who disguised herself and visited Fukazawa village regularly. She made friends with one family, and they began to use her as a baby sitter. After spending quite a while as a model baby sitter, she ate the baby and disappeared!

The villagers were appalled and enraged! They all vowed to wreak vengeance upon her for her terrible deed.

When the ogress eventually came to the village again, the villagers invited her to partake of some delicious-looking dumplings. She gobbled them down with relish. The villager's secret was this: hidden in the center of each dumpling was a red-hot stone. The ogress began to complain that her stomach hurt. When she could no longer stand the pain, she asked for some water. The villagers poured boiling oil into her mouth instead of the water. Wracked with terrible pain, she ran to the river to drink some of the cool water. The heavy stones in her stomach weighted her down and she drowned.

The villagers were happy to be rid of her, but still afraid that she might curse them from her watery grave, so they erected a small shrine beside the river that still remains.

Gyokuzan (1843–1923) was ordained a Buddhist priest, but from the age of 24, he devoted himself exclusively to carving. He was known for his *okimono* of frogs, snakes, crabs, monkeys, and other animals. His netsuke were especially admired. Of the many awards he received, the most important was the Prix d'honneur (for a netsuke depicting a skull) that was presented by HIH Prince Yoshihisa of Kitashirakawa in the presence of Emperor Meiji.

Plate 27

Subject: Boys Practicing Sumo Wrestling
Artist: Unsigned
Material: Boxwood
Date: Nineteenth century
Size: 1 1/2" x 1 5/8" x 1 "

American baseball has gained great popularity in Japan. The best native Japanese players are national heroes. European soccer is spreading across the world and is also played in Japan. Japanese judo, karate, aikido, and *kyudo* are being introduced worldwide in the opposite direction. But sumo, the traditional Japanese style of wrestling remains uniquely Japanese.

Sumo has been practiced in Japan for some 2,000 years. The modern arena in which sumo bouts are staged is a great hall seating over 10,000 spectators. Every aspect of sumo is governed by ancient traditions. The ring itself is built up from the floor and is about 12 feet in diameter. A shrine roof floats over the ring, and a Shinto priest presides at the ceremonial opening of the event. The ring is blessed and each wrestler purifies the ring before entering it for the match by tossing salt into the air.

The ring itself is marked by a large rope that is half buried in the clay mound. Outside the first ring is another half buried rope. The winner is judged as the wrestler who forces the other to touch the surface of the mound with his hands, knees, or any other part, or to be thrown, pushed, or lifted outside of the ring. Since the mound is only slightly larger than the ring, the loser is often thrown off of the mound as well as out of the ring. There is a strict order to the hierarchy, which is controlled by the number of match wins and tournament wins. Each win adds to the amount of money that the winner is awarded.

The sumo wrestlers are large. Some of them look fat, but underneath the flab are strong muscles with which they can lift an equally heavy opponent. In Tokyo, there are three major tournaments each year, one during the New Year holidays, one in May, and one in September. The winner of the tournament gets to keep the "Emperor's Cup" until the next round.

Even this most Japanese of sports is beginning to be enjoyed in the West. Sumo wrestlers have given demonstrations in many countries. In 1990 a sumo tournament was held in Brazil.

Plate 28

Subject: Okame with Fan
Artist: Rantei
Material: Ivory
Date: ca. 1795
Size: 1 1/4" x 3/4" x 1 1/4"

The Shinto goddess of mirth and sensuality is known as Okame, but her real name is Ame no Uzume no Mikoto. She is always shown with these puffy cheeks, a smiling face, and a tiny mouth. This character appears in Noh dramas and other Japanese arts. She is also known to perform provocative dances wherein she displays her more than ample charms.

She is a favorite of netsuke carvers, and is shown both as a full figure and as an Okame mask.

In one legend, the Sun Goddess decided to hide in a cave after being insulted by her brother, the Storm God. She closed the opening of the cave with a giant boulder and thus plunged the earth into darkness. A huge mirror was forged and a string of 500 jewels was hung outside of the cave. Then Okame came and began a particularly sensual dance. The myriad of deities gathered burst into laughter at once. The Sun Goddess then poked her head out of the cave to see what was going on. Seeing her image in the mirror, she emerged further. Just then, a very strong god rolled the giant boulder back into place and she returned to the world again. Thus, Okame is credited with returning daylight to the world.

This character is also used to represent many of the facets of womanhood. She has several names, each one with attributes which are appropriate for that character. She is known as Uzume, Okame, and as Otafuku.

Rantei (fl. 1789–1800) lived in Kyoto and carved mainly ivory. Although he carved animals, flowers, birds and even landscapes, he reached perfection in figure carving. At the request of Prince Ninnaji, he carved a nut with 1,000 monkeys on it. Each one was so tiny that they could not be clearly seen with the unaided eye.

BORDERS

BOOKS MUSIC AND CAFE

98 Buchanan Street
Glasgow G1 Scotland

STORE: 0283   REG: 09/52   TRAN#: 7904
SALE   13/07/2001   EMP: 07372

RETSHKE

        5294944   OP T   14.95

1 Item   Total   14.95
            CASH   20.00
            CASH   3.05-

        13/07/2001 01:30PM

    THANK YOU FOR SHOPPING AT BORDERS
    PLEASE ASK ABOUT OUR SPECIAL EVENTS

        Vat No: 450072771

Plate 29

Subject: Boy on an Ox
Artist: Jugyoku
Material: Ivory
Date: Mid-nineteenth century
Size: 1 5/8" x 1 1/4" x 1 1/4"

The ox is the animal sign for the second year of the Japanese zodiac. Being born in the year of the ox is considered very lucky, and every year of the ox is a lucky year. Perhaps even Wall Street knew of this tradition when naming a prosperous year a "Bull Market." As a draft animal, it embodies agricultural plenty. Small images of oxen were often worn by merchants to ensure continued prosperity.

The ox and its herdsman are a recurring theme in Zen Buddhist art, the *Ten Ox-Herding Songs* being a metaphor for the various stages of enlightenment. Another expression is that the search for Buddhahood is like looking for an ox while riding on its back. Thus, the ox becomes a talisman of wealth, a symbol of deep spiritual meaning, and a noble farm animal.

The ox is the emblem of the God of calligraphy, Tenjin-sama, the deified scholar Sugawara no Michizane. The time of the ox is between 1 and 3 A.M.

A child seated on the back of an ox and playing on a flute is a symbol of complete peace and is a frequent theme in Japanese art. In this netsuke, too, the feeling conveyed is one of peace and contentment.

Jugyoku I (fl. 1848–53), a pupil of the famous Ryukei, excelled in his use of ivory tinting, an art adapted for netsuke by his teacher, Ryukei.

Jugyoku II (fl. 1850–80), a pupil of Keigyoku, was a master of carving both wood and ivory.

This netsuke is thought to be the work of Jugyoku I.

Plate 30

Subject: Mice and Religious Mallet
Artist: Unsigned
Material: Ivory
Date: Twentieth century
Size: 1 7/8" x 1 1/4" x 1 1/4"

The mouse, or rat, is the animal symbol for the first sign of the Oriental zodiac, its time lasting from eleven at night until one in the morning. It is also linked with Daikoku, the God of wealth, one of the Seven Gods of Good Fortune.

There is a legend that certain ancient idols wished to get rid of Daikoku because he was receiving prayers and incense instead of themselves. They asked the God of the Underworld, Emma-O, to send his most clever *oni* to get Daikoku out of the way. Led by a sparrow, the *oni* went to Daikoku's home, but couldn't find him there. After a long search, Daikoku was discovered sitting comfortably on the bales of rice in a great merchant's house. The *oni* hid so that he could take Daikoku by surprise. But his intended victim had heard footsteps and sent his chief rat to see who had come in. The rat discovered the *oni* and ran into the garden for a twig of holly with which he drove the terrified demon back to the gates of hell.

Daikoku's mallet is the Japanese equivalent of Aladdin's lamp. It provides luck and wealth to the wielder at each stroke of its use.

This beautiful ivory netsuke portrays both of the attributes of Daikoku, thus bringing wealth and good fortune to the bearer.

Plate 31

Subject: Mouse
Artist: Kangyoku
Material: Ivory
Date: Mid-1970s
Size: 1 7/8" x 1 5/8" x 1 3/8"

The mouse is a cute animal in Japanese folklore, as it often is in Western tales. One popular children's song has the lyrics:

> The bales of rice are piled so high
> The storehouse is filled full of rice,
> Filled to overflowing with rice;
> The mice squeak and squeal and smile in
> delight;
> And the stars above all twinkle bright,
> Filling the evening sky with shining light.

The rat and the mouse are often confused in Japanese texts because they both are written with the character that reads *nezumi* in Japanese. People born in the zodiac year of the rat are creative and charming. The rat is an emblem of good luck, a symbol of fertility, and a companion of the god of wealth, Daikoku.

The contemporary carver Kangyoku continues in the tradition of creating netsuke that are softly formed and executed with an excellence of technique. He also builds on that tradition of injecting humor, whimsy, or a little twist to the tale that the netsuke represents.

Plate 32

Subject: Fisherman with Octopus
Artist: Unsigned
Material: Ivory
Date: Early nineteenth century
Size: 4 3/16" x 1 1/8" x 1 1/8"

Japan is often referred to as an island nation. It is made up of four main islands and many smaller ones. The oceans that surround the Japanese archipelago are fertile fishing grounds. Since there is relatively little land area and a huge supply of produce from the seas, much of the Japanese diet is composed of seafood.

The reliance on seafood has created many ceremonies that relate to obtaining safe voyages and bountiful catches. One of those interesting ceremonies is the First Casting of the Nets. It is usually done in the beginning of February. A Shinto priest presides over this solemn ceremony. The nets are blessed and then cast into the sea. If there are any fish caught in the nets, it is a good omen. But, as this is not a working day, the lucky fish are returned to the sea unharmed.

Although most Westerners might not think that an octopus is any more edible than a jellyfish, the Japanese enjoy eating both. The octopus tentacles provide firm muscular meat, but if it is not prepared properly it can be chewed on for hours without damaging the tentacle.

This netsuke shows a happy fisherman returning with his catch for the day. This long, narrow style of netsuke is called a *sashi* netsuke; it is inserted behind the *obi* from the top, leaving the head jutting over the top of the belt with the cords that secure the bundle dangling over the front. This style of netsuke gives the owner quick access to the entire set when they must be removed.

Plate 33

Subject: Bonsai Masters
Artist: Kunimitsu
Material: Ivory
Date: 1970s
Size: Standing, 2″ x 1¹/₄″ x 1¹/₄″
　　　 Sitting, 1⁵/₈″ x 1¹/₄″ x 1¹/₄″

Bonsai is one of the Japanese arts that has spread the fastest in the West. There is something basic in human nature that thrills at the idea of capturing a mature tree within a tiny space. These bonsai are not tortured. They are carefully cultivated to keep them healthy. They can only be trained into the artistic styles often seen if they are healthy. In fact, many bonsai live longer under the watchful eye of a loving bonsai gardener than they would in nature, where they are subjected to the changes of the weather in addition to many pests and diseases.

The bonsai gardener creates a plant that can live well in the container by encouraging the formation of tiny fibrous roots to replace the long roots usually required to seek out water. The design of the bonsai is created by pruning away unnecessary branches and guiding those remaining so that they grow into the form desired. Constant attention is required during the growing season to make sure that the branches are developing in the proper directions. To accomplish that, leaf buds are left in the direction growth is wanted, and pruned off from the other areas. Similar techniques are used to shape trees in gardens.

A bonsai requires daily attention. One famous Japanese actor would only accept roles that were within walking distance of his home so that he could attend to his bonsai. He specialized in miniature bonsai, usually under three inches tall, as is the one shown here. Plants growing in that small a container require watering frequently—in summer up to 7 times a day!

In the West, bonsai is frequently a solitary hobby. However, in Japan, it is common to see two or more people working on trimming, repotting, or styling their bonsai together. With land at such a premium in Japan, it is fascinating to notice bonsai growing in containers on balconies, ledges, and rooftops.

The miniature azalea (*var. chinzan*) bonsai shown here, was created by Mr. Larry Williams of Atlanta, Georgia. As one of the pioneers of bonsai in America, Mr. Williams has encouraged many neophytes to achieve their greatest potential in this horticultural art form by researching bonsai training techniques and developing new techniques of his own for refining the form of a bonsai. He has generously shared those techniques with anyone who asked to help improve the quality of bonsai in America. One of the bonsai that he created is in the bonsai collection at the U.S. National Arboretum in Washington, D.C.

Plate 34

Subject: Pigeon in a Freshwater Clam Shell
Artist: Hidemasa
Material: Ivory
Date: ca. 1800
Size: $^7/_8$" x 1 $^{13}/_{16}$" x $^3/_4$"

There are many carvings of clam shells among netsuke and *okimono*. Many of them are shown closed, and they are often assembled in a pile to create a composition similar to the ginkgo nuts shown in Plate 9. The majority of the remaining ones are partially open as this one is, but they usually contain a scene that represents a religious paradise. This is the only netsuke that we have discovered with a bird inside a clam shell.

It is obvious that carving anything inside of a pair of solid walls, with only a slight opening, presents difficulties. It becomes a challenge and an opportunity for the carver to show his skill.

Here is one story about a pigeon that has been told to millions of children in Japan. You can imagine the possibilities for variations on this traditional theme.

In a time long ago, a boy pigeon was a really contrary young bird. If his mother said to go to the mountains, he would go to the river. If his mother said to go to the river, he would go to the garden to work.

His mother always enjoyed the quiet of the mountainside. She decided that, after she died, she would like to be buried there. But she saw how her son always did exactly the opposite of what she wanted. So, when she was very sick, and thought that she might die, she asked him to make her grave along the rocky edge of the river, instead of the mountain-side where she really wished to be buried.

After his mother died, the young boy realized how wrong it was for him to always disobey his mother. So, for the first time, he did just as his mother had said and made her grave in the rocks along the edge of the river. Then came the spring rains, and the river began to fill up and endanger his mother's grave.

And that is why even now in Japan, they say that the pigeon coos whenever it is about to rain, because he is crying for his mother. Thus, it would have been better if he had started obeying his mother a little sooner.

Plate 35

Subject: Boy with a Lion-Dance Mask
Artist: Unsigned
Material: Hirado Porcelain
Date: Twentieth century
Size: 2 3/8" x 1 1/4" x 1 1/4"

One of the oldest traditional Japanese dances is the lion dance. Masks are used to give the viewer an appropriate feeling of awe. Lion dances (*shishi mai)* have been performed since ancient times. Originally, they were danced by one man in a big lion mask with a movable jaw. He created his own accompaniment by beating the rhythm on a little drum.

Later, the dance became more intricate and was performed by a group of dancers and musicians, in the form of a procession through the streets. During the festival of the New Year, bands of *shishi mai* performers roamed the streets visiting each house. The custom served to exorcise evil spirits from the house. Another application of the *shishi mai* has been at festivals and in connection with certain Buddhist rituals. The *shishi mai* was so popular that it even appears in Noh drama and in Kabuki.

The lion dance is the highlight of the Noh drama entitled *Shakkyo*, or the story of the Stone Bridge. The actor wears a wig of shocking red hair that may even reach to the floor. In the climatic scene, he does a dramatic dance on a brocade-covered dais decorated with peonies, the correlation being that the Japanese regard the lion as the king of beasts and the peony as the king of flowers.

This unusual porcelain netsuke shows the lion mask perhaps being used in a New Year children's game. Or it could also be a representation of the child lion in the popular Kabuki favorite *Renjishi.* It was made in the kiln of Lord Matsura in Hirado, an island near Nagasaki. The subject was popular, and there are other similar pieces.

Plate 36

Subject: Lion Dancer
Artist: Unsigned
Material: Ivory
Date: Nineteenth century
Size: 1 5/8" x 1 5/8" x 1 1/8"

Images of lions *(shishi)* were often erected to serve as guardians at the entrances of shrines and temples, where lion dances are still performed to entertain the gods enshrined within. But lion dancers were not always jovial fellows.

An anonymous Noh drama entitled *Mochizuki* tells of how a certain samurai lord, Yasuda Tomoharu, exchanged harsh words with Mochizuki Akinaga, who was so incensed that he slew Yasuda and broke up his family. Yasuda's wife fled with her only son, Hanawaka, to an inn on the shore of Lake Biwa, which, unknown to her, was owned by one of her lord's retainers, Ozawa Tomofusa. They recognize each other, however, and talk of the good old days, and are surprised to learn that Mochizuki has just stopped at the inn on his way back to Kyoto. They plan to take revenge. The woman pretends to be a blind minstrel and sings for Mochizuki in his rooms. She and the innkeeper ply the murderer with sake, and Mochizuki, more than a little drunk, asks Tomofusa to do a lion dance for him.

While Tomofusa gets ready, Hanawaka dances with a hand-drum. The innkeeper then comes in attired as a lion dancer, but instead of a mask he wears a white cloth tied around his head and a wig of very long, bright red hair. He starts to dance, and Mochizuki, very drunk by now, reclines in careless abandon. Seeing this, Tomofusa and Hanawaka fall upon him and kill him, thus avenging the wrong he did to the Yasuda family.

The Hirado porcelain netsuke in the previous plate was probably created from a mold, with some additional hand work to the clay and then the glaze was applied by hand also. In this ivory carving, everything is the hand work of the artist.

The finest netsuke are unique pieces. Each one is created under the inspiration of a netsuke master. Carving is not the only technique used, but it is the most frequent technique. Fine quality netsuke have also been created through metalworking, lacquerwork and other techniques.

Plate 37

Subject: Puppy with Sea Shell
Artist: Unsigned
Material: Ivory
Date: Mid-nineteenth century
Size: ⁵/₁₆" x 2 ³/₈" x 1 "

The dog is the animal symbol of the eleventh year of the Oriental zodiac. There are several types of native Japanese dogs—Akita, Tosa, Kai, Kishu, Koshi, Ainu, etc.

The dog is a friendly character in Japanese stories, folklore, and literature, a beneficent and protective character. In *Momotaro (The Little Peachling)*, a Japanese fairy tale, a dog is one of Momotaro's faithful companions and aids in his successful campaign against the ogres. The dog and the lion guard many temples and shrines in Japan. In the Harima mountains there is even a Buddhist temple called *Inu-dera,* "Dog Temple."

However, in a book by Lady Sei Shonagon written between 991 and 1000 A.D., she relates an incident in which a dog was exiled because it barked at a cat that had been honored with court ranking.

It is believed that chanting *inu-no-ko, inu-no-ko* ("puppy, puppy") will make a baby quiet when it cries while sleeping. A papier-mâché puppy, much like the one in this netsuke is dangled over the crib for the protection of babies. Placing the ideograph for "dog" on a child's forehead is done to drive away the demons of disease. A papier-mâché dog is sometimes placed near a woman in labor because dogs are known for their easy delivery.

Shogun Tsunayoshi was so fond of dogs that he was affectionately known as *Inu-Kubo*—the Dog Prince.

Plate 38

Subject: Gourd Group
Artist: Gyokuso
Material: Boxwood
Date: Early twentieth century
Size: ³/₄" x 1 ⁵/₁₆" x ¹⁵/₁₆"

Sometimes the netsuke carver chooses subjects that appeal to him purely for their sculptural quality. This piece and the group of ginkgo seeds (*see* Plate 9) are two that fall into that category. This tiny group of gourds has a powerful abstract quality to it. If this work of art had been executed in the same proportions, but in equivalent meters or yards in length, it would be comparable in strength to a Henry Moore sculpture.

One of the challenges that many forms of Japanese art provides us is learning how to see things on a whole new scale. Bonsai—live miniature trees—are another example. Most bonsai are less than two feet tall. Many are only a few inches tall (*see* Plate 33), yet each one is a work of art unto itself. The Japanese aesthetic is geared to creating the most impact in the least amount of space.

The Japanese garden utilizes very few elements and is usually impeccably maintained to give the viewer more enjoyment from the small space employed than is usually attained in sweeping Western landscaping. It takes a special awareness of the beauty in understatement to appreciate much of Japanese art. The tea ceremony and Japanese flower arrangement are two more examples of the Japanese minimalist aesthetic.

Gyokuso was born in 1879 and lived until nearly the mid-point of the twentieth century (1944). He is identified with the Tokyo school of netsuke carvers. Other similar style carvings of his include a group of peanuts, two clams, a tangerine, and five eggplants. It may be difficult for us to assess his true carving skill today because these forms are so simplified. They are monumental, yet miniature sculptures.

His exceptional combination of design sense and carving proficiency is shown in other netsuke, such as a boat with a man, a rabbit with a *tanuki*, or a ferry boat with seven people in it!

Plate 39

Subject: Noh Mask of an Old Man *(Shojo)*
Artist: Hideyuki
Material: Ivory
Date: Nineteenth century
Size: 2 1/8" x 1 3/8" x 1 1/8"

In his classic book on Japanese legends, Henri L. Joly lists 138 masks used in various Noh dramas. The purpose of the mask is to preserve the visual identity of the character so that any performer can act out the role while the costume and the mask serve to identify the character instantly. The masks are usually stylized or have exaggerated features so that the character can be easily recognized.

The traditional masks are superb works of art, most of which are still treasured by the theatrical troupes or are in the collections of museums. In the exhibit at the Tokyo National Museum covering the arts of the Muromachi period, ten masks were included along with other works of art such as paintings, sculptures, and ceramics. The masks shown dated from the fourteenth and fifteenth centuries. When the Japanese government sent an exhibition of art works to the United States in 1989 to show the development of Japanese arts over the period from 1185 to 1868, they included fifteen masks.

As impressive as the full size masks are in person, the netsuke masks are even more so. The netsuke artist has been able to convey the same dramatic character in a carving that is less than two inches tall and that occupies only 1/16 the area of the full-sized mask. Such netsuke are so powerful that some collectors specialize in collecting masks.

Many netsuke artists have used the name Hideyuki. One contemporary netsuke carver uses the name Kosei Hideyuki for this reason. In Japan, it has been a tradition for artists in all fields to adopt the name of previous masters of their art. Sometimes, the name is given by the master for his best student to use. In Japanese theater, the artistic names of the finest actors have been passed on from generation to generation in some families for over 200 years. Other artists adopt an artistic name of their own choosing. It may be chosen because of an admiration for a previous artist's work, an affinity of style or subject matter, or just a fondness for the name.

Plate 40

Subject: South Seas Coral Diver
Artist: Unsigned
Material: Ebony
Date: Late eighteenth century
Size: 2 5/16" x 1 1/8" x 5/8"

Most Westerners see the Japanese islands as a series of dots in the northwest corner of the Pacific Ocean. Therefore, it is difficult to realize that the Japanese islands extend in a graceful arc that is situated in the same latitudes as the east coast of North America, stretching as though from Nova Scotia to the Bahamas. Consequently, there is a great range in temperature throughout the nation. The winters are severe on the northern island of Hokkaido, where the 1972 Winter Olympics were held in Sapporo. Even the southernmost main island, Kyushu, gets a little snowfall each winter; but the Ryukyu chain of Okinawa is semi-tropical, like the West Indies, and attracts lots of winter tourists trying to escape the snowy north.

This early netsuke is of a South Seas coral diver returning to the surface with a piece of branched coral (which might eventually be carved into one or more netsuke and *ojime*). The carver has used a dark wood in order to portray a dark-skinned native of the South Seas.

Many netsuke of divers portray *ama,* the female divers who usually wear only a loincloth and carry a sharp knife for harvesting pearls or abalone. One favorite subject is an *ama* with an amorous octopus, as is also seen in an ukiyo-e by Hokusai. Divers are also portrayed in other Japanese arts. A Noh drama by Zeami (1363–1443), *Ama,* tells about a pearl diver who sacrificed herself to assure her son's success.

Since many netsuke were carved on commission, here is one possible explanation for the creation of this coral diver netsuke.

A wealthy merchant from northern Hokkaido decided to spend his winter vacation on the southern island of Okinawa, much like the many people from Michigan who are found in Florida during January. He enjoyed the lush tropical foliage, the fresh fruit, and swimming in the ocean. He frequently visited the fisherman to see the peculiar shapes and brilliant colors of the fish that they caught which were much more exotic than the fish from his northern waters. When he was about to return home, one of the divers presented him with a large piece of coral as a souvenir. He placed it in a prominent spot in his home in a special alcove called a *tokonoma.* However, he could not enjoy the piece of coral because he was away from home all day, and often late into the night, due to his work. One day he realized that he always took his netsuke, *ojime,* and inro with him, so he commissioned a local carver to create this netsuke. Then, no matter how severe the winter weather became, all he had to do was to reach down to his *obi* and touch his coral diver netsuke to instantly re-enjoy the warm ocean breezes of his vacation.

Plate 41

Subject: Shishi
Artist: Mitsumasa
Material: Ivory
Date: 1815
Size: 1 3/4" x 1 1/2" x 1 "

The Chinese guardian lions are called *shih-tzu.* In Japanese, they are the popular *shishi.* They are usually shown playing with a ball, or one of their young. When they are created in pairs, the male frequently has one front foot resting on the ball, and the female has her opposite front foot resting on one of her cubs. The male usually has his mouth open, and the female mouth is closed, symbolizing yin and yang. In paintings, they are sometimes shown romping through peonies or playing with a sacred gem.

The *shishi* had to be fierce and tough to be guardians. Legend tells that they would test the strength and endurance of their young by throwing them off of a cliff. Those that returned were sure to be long lived and trustworthy guardians.

One method of amusement from ancient times was playing the "Game of the Lion." In this dance, two men would wear a lion costume and dance in unison, while a third would play with a large ball in front of them. The ball may represent a precious gem that the lion is seeking, the sun, the dual powers of nature (yin and yang), or a symbolic egg.

Shishi are rarely shown as in this netsuke, hatching from a giant egg.

Not much is written about the carver Mitsumasa. Judging from subject and style, he was a member of the Nagoya school of Ittan.

Plate 42

Subject: Monkey Trainer
Artist: Unsigned
Material: Ivory
Date: Nineteenth century
Size: 2 7/8" x 2 1/2" x 1 7/16"

In ancient times, monkeys were dressed in coats and hats to entertain the laborers on Imperial projects. Because they performed such an important function, the monkey trainers were allowed to roam the country. They were one of the few people that could travel between rival regional lands. They made ideal spies, and many Japanese dramas and stories feature treacherous monkey trainers.

In one twist of such a tale, the great fourteenth-century military strategist Masashige used this freedom to his advantage. In 1332, Masashige was defending a fort against an overwhelming number of attackers. The rival army was successful at blockading the fort and stopped the flow of provisions into it. Masashige built a large bonfire and spread the rumor that it was his funeral pyre. However, he and the majority of his troops escaped in the dark of night, leaving only a few to light the fire.

The attacking general saw the blaze and succeeded in capturing the unmanned fort. Perceiving no additional problems, he left the fort lightly guarded and returned to his other campaigns. Masashige sent one of his generals to spy on the fort, dressed as a monkey trainer. The disguise worked and he discovered that a convoy of supplies was due to arrive soon. Masashige intercepted the convoy, hid his troops in the wagons and thereby regained entrance to the fort without any further loss of life. The guard troops then joined with his forces.

Another story of a monkey trainer can be found in the Kyogen play filled with the warmth of human kindness, entitled *Utsubo-zaru* (The Monkey-skin Quiver). In it, a Daimyo goes hunting with his servant. They meet a monkey trainer. The Daimyo is greatly impressed with the beauty of the monkey's fur, and wants to use it for his arrow quiver. When the trainer refuses to part with his monkey, the Daimyo becomes enraged and threatens to kill both of them. The trainer then agrees to kill the monkey himself, but instead of shooting it which will damage the skin, he will dispatch it himself with a large stick.

When the trainer raises the stick, the monkey takes it as a signal to perform and grabs the stick. The trainer bursts into tears at this complete obedience in the face of danger. The Daimyo is greatly moved, and decides not to kill either of them. In gratitude, the monkey dances to the trainer's songs and the Daimyo is so touched that he begins to dance with the monkey, thus ending on a happy note.

Plate 43

Subject: Mythical Creature, the *Kirin*
Artist: Tomotada
Material: Wood
Date: Late eighteenth century
Size: 4 3/8" x 1 1/2" x 7/8"

The Oriental *kirin* is similar to the Western unicorn. It is a magical creature that does no harm and is a very auspicious symbol. There are many varieties of *kirins*.

The *kirin* is an imaginary animal from China where it is called *ch'i-lin*. It never even bends a blade of grass while walking because it is bound to avoid injury to any living thing. It has the body of a stag, one horn, the tail of a cow, and the hoofs of a horse. It has a yellow belly, and is adorned with five colors of hair (compare this *kirin* to the one depicted on a bottle of Kirin beer).

The *kirin* is usually wrapped in flames. In Chinese mythology, the *kirin* ranks above the dragon, whereas in Japan, the dragon is predominant.

The *kirin* embodies the virtues of goodness and grace. Its appearance is believed to presage the coming of a great sage or ruler. It is supposed to be voiceless, but it is often depicted in netsuke as though calling to the moon.

This rendering of the *kirin* is typical of the style that Tomotada (fl. 1781–1800) popularized. He was very successful in his own time. He was especially gifted at carving in wood, and many of his designs were freely reproduced by other carvers of his own time and later.

Plate 44

Subject: Pair of Cranes
Artist: Bishu
Material: Ivory
Date: 1970s
Size: 2" x 1 7/8" x 1 1/8"

The crane is held in great honor in Japan. *Grus japonica* is the national bird of Japan and appears on the currency. It is one of the symbols of longevity. Crane designs are often used to decorate the magnificent wedding kimono because cranes mate for life. Thus they impart a double blessing for a long life and a long marriage. This double *tsuru* netsuke has a pair of cranes joined forever.

In the Taoist system, the crane stands for the heavenly principle, forming the foundation of the universe, while the earthly principle is represented by the tortoise. Both are characteristic inhabitants of the holy mountain, Horai.

In feudal times, one of the sports of the samurai was to hunt cranes with hawks. It would seem impossible for a hawk to capture a crane, since cranes are over five feet tall. Yet it was a regular event. One such hawk hunter learned a lesson from a crane. His valiant hawk had captured a crane and forced it to the ground. When the samurai approached the crane to kill it, it did not move but stared back at him. The hawk-hunter was so impressed by this "samurai-like way" of accepting the inevitable that he gave up hunting cranes.

Cranes used to gather in huge flocks, but as the Japanese economy has grown, much of their native habitat has been destroyed. The cranes summer in China and return to Japan for the winter. Their arrival in late fall is heralded with many festivals. Today, their flocks are increasing, because they are protected and have become an important tourist attraction.

This netsuke shows the genius of Bishu as a twentieth-century netsuke artist. It is a perfectly formed netsuke in all of the traditional requirements—smooth outline, compact form, sturdy composition and materials. Yet, the design itself and the use of pure, unstained material are the epitome of twentieth-century netsuke art.

(*See* pp. 30–36 for more information about Bishu.)

Plate 45

Subject: Crane
Artist: Shingetsu
Material: Ivory
Date: Late twentieth century
Size: 1 ³/₄" x 1 ¹/₄" x ⁷/₈"

The crane is called *tsuru* and is regarded as sacred. It is a large bird, standing five feet tall. In areas where the cranes live in Japan, the people have developed a respect and care for them. The children are told to "behave like the *tsuru*" because cranes never fight over food, are well mannered in all other ways as well, and mate for life. If one crane becomes sick or crippled, the mate will remain with it, even through the winter. Caring people find the birds and provide food and shelter for them. Otherwise they would die.

Another reason for wanting children to behave like *tsuru* is that the crane's children always walk, hop, or fly politely behind their parents.

The sacred crane was encouraged to inhabit the grounds of the feudal lords to bring them good luck. When the cranes migrated, or the lords fortunes migrated, cranes of cast iron were substituted in their gardens.

The crane remains today a popular symbol of peace. Paper cranes folded in the origami style are often offered by the thousands at shrines for peace.

Shingetsu (b. 1934) is the fourth son of the ivory sculptor Manjiro Muramatsu, who used the artistic name of Kogyokyu. Shingetsu is one of the few contemporary netsuke artists who combines traditional subjects and techniques with the vigor of contemporary design. He is especially skilled in the use of lacquer, which he learned from the lacquer artist Tatsuaki Kuroda, who has been designated as a Living National Treasure by the Japanese government.

Some of his work is highly lacquered, while other pieces may contain only a blush of color. His work expresses the finest qualities of contemporary netsuke—bold designs impeccably rendered.

Plate 46

Ojime
Subject: Zodiac Signs of the Dog and the Dragon
Artist: Naokazu
Material: Ivory
Date: ca. 1840
Size: $^5/_8$" x $^3/_4$" x $^5/_8$"

The dragon and the dog are the fifth and the eleventh animals of the Oriental zodiac cycle. When they are portrayed together, they represent the fifth hours of the morning (7 to 9 A.M.) and evening (7 to 9 P.M.) of the Japanese day.

The dragon has a number of remarkable attributes: for instance, it can change its size at will from one extreme to another, and can even become invisible. Its breath becomes a cloud from which water or fire rains. In the Orient, it usually has more to do with water than with fire, and often appears in the clouds. But even this powerful creature, has enemies, and one of these is the centipede. It is frightened of five-colored silk and does not like iron. It is devoted to the Buddha and his followers, and is often shown in their company.

The dragon represents the essence of life exhibited through its unending ability to adapt to all circumstances, in all times, and in all surroundings, like the continuous cycles of life.

From prehistoric times, dogs have played an important role in human activities in Japan. Dog lore has been widespread, especially among hunters and farmers, and a dog cult, related to the wolf cults of northeastern Asia arose.

There are several native Japanese breeds of dogs. They are all regarded as good watchdogs, being always faithful and devoted to their masters. A true story about canine loyalty is that of Hachiko. For many years, Hachiko, a native Akita breed dog, would come to the Shibuya Station and wait for his master to return from work. After his master's death in 1925, Hachiko loyally went to his position near the station exit every day and waited until the last train had arrived. He continued for many years, and the dog became renowned for his loyal perseverance.

He became so loved by the people of the area that, after his death, a portrait statue of Hachiko was erected near where he had so faithfully awaited his master.

Koryusai Naokazu (fl. 1830–43) carved masterfully well in both ivory and wood. He was quite renowned as a carver of figures with intricate details.

Plate 47

Subject: Tiger and Dragon
Artist: Unsigned
Material: Silver, Gold, and Ivory
Date: Possibly early eighteenth century
Size: 2" diameter x 1/2"

This *kagami-buta* style netsuke is probably the earliest netsuke in this book. Although it is unsigned, netsuke experts have dated this piece from between the end of the seventeenth century to the mid-eighteenth century by comparing the quality of the workmanship and the metalworking techniques utilized to known pieces. Yet many neophyte collectors would not have been tempted to buy this netsuke because it is unsigned. That is why it is so important to develop your own eye for quality. And it is especially important if you enjoy these *manju*-style netsuke, as they are almost never signed. Whatever art you enjoy, you should experience it as frequently as possible so that you become intimately familiar with its nuances.

In this metalworking technique, gold was affixed to the base metal by applying heat, rather than by using electricity as is done today.

Together, the tiger and the dragon represent the major powers of the Buddhist faith. The tiger is the greatest terrestrial power, and the dragon, the preeminence in the celestial sphere. The breath of the tiger is the wind, and the breath of the dragon is water. They are the irresistible force and the immovable object of the East. Another tiger/dragon relationship is that the dragon represents the forces of nature and the tiger represents the strongest animal on earth. This *manju* (rice-cake form) netsuke depicts this classic confrontation. The tiger is rendered in gold and the dragon in silver.

Plate 48

Subject: Toad
Artist: Masanao
Material: Wood
Date: Nineteenth century
Size: $7/8$" x $1 5/8$" x 1"

English-language translations of Japanese folktales are imprecise in their usage of the terms toad and frog. They are often used interchangeably. In the West, toads are land creatures that have bumpy skins, and frogs are water creatures with smooth skins. In Japanese, there are many descriptions of bumpy skinned amphibians called "frogs."

One exception is that of the Toad Sage, or *Gama Sennin*. Nearly always, this sage is shown accompanied by toads. He is said to possess magical powers, one of which is a magical pill that gives 100 years of life.

Another supernatural power attributed to toads is that they are able to disappear completely when there seems to be no possible way out of a situation. There is even a saying that you can keep a toad in a bamboo basket, but not in a wooden box. The origin of this saying comes from observing that toads will squeeze through seemingly impossibly small holes, such as one might find in an old wooden box, if there is only one way to get out. But if a toad is put in a basket, it first tries one gap and then another, always looking for a hole that is large enough for it to fit through comfortably. Not finding one, it therefore stays trapped.

In one Japanese legend, the robber Tokubei traveled from Japan to India in the 1600s. In the Kabuki play about his life, he is depicted as being surrounded with frogs. Stories of him in both legend and theater say that he escaped his enemies by disguising himself as a frog.

This toad is obviously just waiting for a tasty morsel, and is not at all worried about disappearing at any time soon.

The signature on this wooden netsuke clearly reads "Masanao." The subject matter is a popular creation by Masanao. The question is, which Masanao? The line of netsuke carvers bearing that name stretches back through eight different artists to Suzuki Masanao (1815–90). The contemporary netsuke carver, Shinzan Masanao (1904–82) was a direct descendant of Suzuki Masanao, and his daughter Suzuki Masami now carries on the Masanao tradition. Most of this family's work depicts nature in wood. A tribute to the Japanese system of traditional apprenticeship is that netsuke created by the contemporary Masanao are considered to be comparable to work by the much acclaimed earlier Masanaos from as long as 150 years ago.

Plate 49

Subject: Peach with Chain
Artist: Unsigned
Material: Ivory
Date: Nineteenth century
Size: 1 3/8" x 1 1/8" x 1 "

The Noh play *Tobo-saku* tells the story of the peach as a Taoist symbol of immortality. When a certain emperor in ancient China was celebrating the Star Festival, an old Taoist hermit pointed at a special bird flying overhead and announced that Sei-o-bo (the Great Mother of the Western Paradise) would soon appear, bearing a peach that can be produced only once every three thousand years. The peach can grant immortality to whomever partakes of it.

Later, he reappeared in his true form, the Taoist immortal Tobo-saku, and together with Sei-o-bo, they offered the peach to the emperor and danced in his honor. The same story is told in the popular Noh play entitled *Sei-o-bo.*

The peach is a symbol of femininity. It represents softness, mildness, and peacefulness. It has decided erotic qualities, being the Okame of the fruit world. This particular netsuke has more features to it than one would first imagine.

Of course, anyone can see the large peach and the smaller ones. And there is a monkey, trying as usual to steal the fruit. However, this piece also hides a secret compartment that is entered by unscrewing one of the smaller peaches. The secret that is revealed is a three-inch-long chain attached to the small peach—all carved from the single piece of ivory.

Many netsuke are created just to display these intricate craftsmanship skills. For instance, the ball in the mouth of the boy lion-dancer moves freely (Plate 35); and then there are the two birds in the cage of Kunimitsu's bird vendor (Plate 18).

Plate 50

Subject: Sambaso Dancer
Artist: Dosho
Material: Ivory
Date: Mid-nineteenth century
Size: 1 3/4" x 1 1/2" x 1 1/4"

Plate 51

Subject: Sambaso Dancers
Artist: Unsigned
Material: Ivory
Date: Nineteenth century
Size: Under 2" tall

In the temple city of Nara, a great fissure opened in the ground in the year 807 A.D., belching fire and smoke. A priest was called to rectify the situation and he performed the *Sambaso* dance. The purpose of the dance was to placate the gods.

The costume is precisely delineated, beginning with the unusually tall hat, which is somewhat like a flattened cone. The background is black, with a large red disc centered upon it representing the sun. There are 12 divisions marked on the hat to represent the months. The robes are decorated with exquisite embroidery showing symbols of longevity such as the crane and pine branches.

The performer wears a black mask depicting an old man. He carries a fan in one hand and a ceremonial sistrum of little bells in the other.

The Noh drama is the classic theater of Japan. Performances were originally held in connection with the festivals at shrines and temples. It first received governmental patronage under the Shogun Ashikaga Yoshimitsu (1368–94). Each performance was preceded by the ritual drama *Okina,* which contains a purification dance that was performed by Sambaso to placate the gods and to assure that the performance would be good. Even today, it retains all of the ancient traditions.

Sambaso netsuke always depict this ceremonial dance from the Noh drama. They are a marvel of design, since the dancer is always shown "in motion" with one foot raised. The netsuke must be naturally balanced so that the *Sambaso* dancer can remain poised on one foot–forever.

Dosho (1828–84) studied ivory carving under the master carver Doraku. He used a variety of materials, including wood, bamboo, tortoiseshell, water-buffalo horn, and precious stones. Some contemporary carvers are also starting to carve netsuke from precious and semi-precious stones. The tradition of carving decorative and artistic images from stones is probably universal. The most exquisite miniature carvings from stones and minerals in Western cultures are those prepared for the Russian nobility by the Fabergē studios.

The following pair of netsuke are the ones discussed on page 15.

Plate 52

Subject: Mother Monkey and Two Young
Artist: Masatami
Material: Ivory
Date: Mid-ninteenth century
Size: 1 7/8" x 1 5/8" x 1 5/8"

At Beppu, there is a unique zoo with no cages. It is called Monkey Mountain. The monkeys live in the hills above the town, and regularly descend upon the town in a group to feed on peanuts bought by tourists for this purpose. As though by a signal, all of the monkeys run off at once—leaving visitors to speculate as to which species was the sightseer.

There are several native varieties of monkey in Japan. There is one tribe of monkeys that lives on Japan's northernmost island, Hokkaido. During the majority of the year, they roam freely throughout the hills and mountains. In the winter, they congregate near the hot springs, where they can be found comfortably avoiding winter by sitting in the warm water wearing a crown of snow flakes.

Plate 53

Subject: Mother Monkey and Four Young with a Pomegranate
Artist: Masatami
Material: Ivory
Date: Late nineteenth century
Size: 2" x 1 3/4" x 1 3/4"

The monkey is the animal symbol of the ninth year in the twelve-year signs of the Oriental zodiac, and the pomegranate is the symbol of many descendants. Perhaps this is because the fruit is full of seeds—nearly bursting from the load. Here, the monkey is itself covered with its own young and holding a pomegranate. The combination would make an appropriate gift at a wedding to wish the couple many fruitful years.

This piece is a little too large and heavy to be considered a netsuke. It may be called an *okimono*—a decorative object that is placed in a special area of a room for the appreciation of the owner and guests. There is a fine line between a large netsuke and a small *okimono*. In this case, the weight may be more of a consideration than the size. This type of carving became popular during the late nineteenth century and early twentieth century as styles of clothing were changing in Japan. Men began wearing Western-style clothes, and thus there was less demand for usable netsuke. Many carvers made slightly larger pieces for the enjoyment of the growing number of export customers.

Both of these powerful, evocative pieces were carved by Masatami I, described on page 56.

Plate 54

Subject: Daruma
Artist: Tadatoshi
Material: Boxwood
Date: Late eighteenth century
Size: 1 5/8" x 1 1/16" x 1 "

Daruma, the Japanese rendering of Bodhidharma, was the twenty-eighth Indian patriarch of Zen Buddhism. He was born at the beginning of the sixth century into an Indian royal family. He went to China as a Buddhist missionary, where he became the first Chinese patriarch of Zen Buddhism. Among the many tales of his time in China is this one.

Daruma meditated for nine years in a cave at the Shaolin monastery on Mount Su. He sat for so long that his legs lost all of their strength. When a painter came to the monastery to restore the temple murals, he thought that the meditating Daruma was a weather-beaten statue and decided to restore it also. But when the painter's brush touched Daruma's body, he was able to walk again.

This netsuke depicts Daruma in the form of a doll. Many Daruma dolls are even more stylized than this one. The Daruma doll is a lucky symbol of an undaunted spirit triumphing after many failures. It is designed so that it will always right itself when knocked over. This design comes from Daruma's admonition *Nanakorobi-yaoki* or "Seven times down, eight times up." If you have a worthwhile goal, persevere and you will attain the goal.

In another Daruma-doll tradition, a brightly colored doll with large blank eyes is kept in a prominent place in a business or at home. When a prayer is made, one of the pupils is painted in; only when one's prayer has been answered or a particular goal achieved is the other pupil added. One variation of this tradition has the Japanese businessman painting in one pupil at the onset of a project, and the other to celebrate its completion. In the New Year celebrations, thousands of Daruma dolls are happily thrown into bonfires, acknowledging last year's achievements, and making way for a new Daruma doll and new goals for the New Year.

Tadatoshi, a Nagoya netsuke carver, worked solely in wood and was active from 1781 to 1800. His early style closely followed that of his contemporary Tametaka (Plate 22), but he developed a realistic style of his own. Tadatoshi is known for his excellent netsuke of figures, masks and animals. His signature was usually in the raised character style.

Plate 55

Incense Box
Subject: Rooster
Artist: Unsigned
Material: Lacquer
Date: 1860
Size: 2 7/8" x 1 1/8"

This incense box or *kogo,* is lacquered with an image of the rooster, or cock, which represents the tenth year in the Japanese zodiac cycle. The cock is considered to have five virtues: *faithfulness,* since it always heralds the dawn; *courage,* because it is brave in fighting; *charity,* as it informs others when it has found food; *strength,* as its feet are tough; and *civility,* represented by the comb on its head.

The cock has become a talisman against evil spirits because its calling at daybreak drives away the devils that have been roaming the countryside all night. At the Grand Shrine of Ise, the cock is regarded as a messenger of the Sun Goddess and one is always to be found within the shrine compounds.

The cock has been raised in Japan for a very long time. One of the interesting varieties that has been developed is the long-tailed cock. The tail feathers grow so long that the birds have to be kept on tall perches. The unusual beauty of these birds requires daily attention. They must be taken off the perch and walked every day; all the while, the tail feathers must be held above the ground by an attendant to keep them from getting soiled. By the time the cocks are three years old, they may have 15-feet-long tails. Long-tailed cocks may live to be nine years of age, and their tails may reach as much as thirty feet in length.

A popular scene that is often depicted in paintings and in netsuke is of a cock standing upon a ceremonial drum. The story goes that a special drum was set up in front of the Imperial Palace in China. Whenever the ruler received a letter speaking in opposition to something that had been established by law, the drum was struck. One ruler was so popular that the drum remained unbeaten throughout his entire life. The cocks became used to it and found it a handy perch. Thus, a cock on a drum is the symbol of peace and prosperity in Japan, where no one has cause for complaint.

Plate 56

Subject: Old Princess
Artist: Meikosai
Material: Ivory
Date: Early twentieth century
Size: 1 3/8" x 2 1/4" x 13/16"

Poetry is a very important part of Japanese life. Every year there is a national poetry contest. The winners are honored at a reception with the Emperor at the Imperial Palace. The ceremony is initiated with the reading of a poem composed by the Emperor himself. Thereafter, the winning poems are read.

There has been no sexual discrimination in recognizing great poetry, even from ancient times. One of the most noted poets served the emperors Ninmyo (r. 834–50) and Montoku (r. 851–58). She was the court lady Ono no Komachi. Every account of her mentions her beauty, and the fact that she was the idol of the court. She refused proposals of marriage from all of the young courtiers. Her poetry was greatly honored within her lifetime and has been saved in many books. Her writings have been interpreted by many different artists. A popular series of Japanese wood-block prints (*ukiyo-e*), depict seven scenes from her life.

She so enjoyed poetry and court life that she had hardly blinked an eye when she realized that old age had caught up with her. She is often depicted in this state as a lonely old woman. When she is shown seated upon a wooden post—sometimes also used as a temporary grave marker—it represents her mourning the death of her lover. The Noh play *Sotoba Komachi* is based on this incident.

One poem that she wrote reflecting upon this scene reads:

> The cherry blossoms
> Have passed away, their color lost,
> While to no avail
> Age takes my beauty as it falls
> In the long rain of my regret.

Plate 57

Subject: Rat with a Candle
Artist: Masatami
Material: Ivory
Date: Mid-nineteenth century
Size: 7/8" x 1 5/8" x 7/8"

The rat is the animal symbol for the first year of the twelve-year cycle in the Japanese zodiac. According to legend, when Buddha called the animals to come before him, the rat arrived first, beating the others by jumping on the ox's head and jumping off again just in time to arrive first! Therefore, the rat is the first animal in the zodiac. It is also the messenger of Daikoku, the god of wealth and one of the Seven Gods of Good Fortune. The rat's ability to hoard riches made him a favorite of the merchant class, and therefore of the netsuke artist.

Here, a rat is carrying a candle. Rats are often shown nibbling a candle, which must provide fat for their nutritional needs. The rat obviously has no way to light a candle. Perhaps this is another whimsical look at the human passion for collecting things.

One rat-related tale tells of the old farmer who took some dumplings with him into the field to work. (Japanese dumplings are considerably more delicious than Western ones.) As he was about to enjoy lunch, he accidently dropped one of his dumplings into a hole in the field. He didn't want to loose such a tasty meal, so he chased it down the hole and under the field. There he found many rats, dancing, eating, and having a great party. He shared his dumplings with the rats and they invited him to stay for the party. He was royally entertained by all the party goers.

When the old farmer's neighbor heard about the great party in the rat cavern, he entered the hole, too, but the rats knew that he was there to exploit their hospitality and drove him away.

In some areas, even today, there is a belief that rats will stay in a house as long as the family is prosperous. If the rats leave, it is a sign of impending bad luck, or that the house will soon be destroyed by fire.

For other examples of netsuke carved by Masatami I, *see* Plates 2, 52, and 53.

Plate 58

Subject: A Ni-o as a Sandal Maker
Artist: Jugyoku
Material: Boxwood
Date: Early nineteenth century
Size: 1 1/4" x 1 1/4" x 3/4"

Ni-o are the guardian deities that flank the gates of Buddhist temples. There are separate figures for the right and left sides of the temple gate. The figure on the right represents wisdom and virtue and is masculine in character. His right hand holds a thunderbolt, his left hand is raised with palm open, and his mouth is open. The other figure represents reason and virtue and is feminine in character. His left hand holds a club, his right hand is raised as though to hit something, and his mouth is closed. In addition to guarding the entrances as works of sculpture, the Ni-o are often painted on the doors of the inner temples. Straw sandals are often hung as votive offerings on the railing in front of these paintings, the custom being that such an offering will give the wearer great strength in the legs.

Netsuke often show the Ni-o in association with sandals. Perhaps one reason is that sandal-making was usually reserved for the lowest class of people. The reason for showing a temple guardian engaged in such a task is to emphasize that even a guardian deity will diligently perform menial tasks when needed for the betterment of the faith.

Jugyoku carved many Buddhist subjects as netsuke. Compare this piece with the Boy on an Ox (Plate 29).

Plate 59

Subject: Kyudo, Japanese Archery
Artist: Maroney
Material: Boxwood
Date: 1990
Size: 1 7/8" x 15/16" diameter

Presented on an offering table before the court archers from an Imperial doll set, is a *hikime,* or ceremonial humming bulb tip for a Japanese arrow. The whistling or humming arrow, which had been used to signal troop movements and the start of battle in ancient times, is used today in a Shinto purification ceremony. One contemporary use was in Washington, D.C., in 1988, when 80-year-old Master Archer, Hideharu Onuma performed the Humming-Bulb-Arrow Ceremony at the re-dedication of the cherry trees. The event was in honor of the seventy-fifth anniversary of their donation from the people of Japan to the people of the United States. The ceremony was performed in front of dignitaries from Washington, D.C., and a delegation of nearly 100 high-ranking Japanese archers. Even in Japan, the ceremony is performed only for very special occasions. It is a rare privilege to be in attendance when it is done.

Many aspects of Japanese archery, or *kyudo,* are based on Shinto religious ceremonies and Zen Buddhist concepts. Of course, the origins of *kyudo* stem from a time when hunting accuracy was important. Today, however, in this elegant, ceremonial form of archery the emphasis is on developing concentration, improving physical coordination, enhancing group participation, and achieving an integrated lifestyle.

Whereas there are over a million people practicing *kyudo* in Japan, and there are several thousand in Europe, there are less than two hundred in North America.

Mr. Maroney, an emerging American netsuke carver, attended the Washington, D.C. Humming-Bulb-Arrow Ceremony. The sound of the whistling arrow was so inspirational, that he created this *hikime* netsuke.

Plate 60

Subject: Rotting Pear and Flower
Artist: Koetsu
Material: Ivory
Date: Late twentieth century
Size: Pear, 2" x 1⁷/₈" x 1⁷/₈"
$\qquad$ Flower, 1³/₄" x 1⁷/₈" x 1⁷/₈"

The pear with its *ukibori* carving and the unfolding flower petals seem to require two different skills, yet each netsuke is unmistakably by the same carver as can be seen by his characteristic inset insects.

Japan is a mountainous country. Some 80% of the land is not easily developed, and therefore not heavily populated. Yet, throughout these areas, many people live and farm small plots. In those remote areas, there is little call of modern "conveniences" such as refrigeration. On many Buddhist and Shinto holidays, offerings of food are placed on the family alters or brought to the shrines and temples. In these ways, even today, one can find a flower or an overripe pear sitting on an offertory table, un-refrigerated, with perhaps an insect or two performing the duty of carrying the nectar to the gods.

A descendant of a samurai family, Koetsu Okazaki was born in Tokyo in 1935. His netsuke and *okimono* subjects in ivory include fruit, flowers, and dragons, as well as humorous subjects such as two frogs playing golf on a lily pad. He is very adept at using inlay as well as lacquer, and his recent pieces are quite elaborate and colorful. He is President of the Japan Ivory Carvers' Association at present.

Plate 61

Subject: Skull and Snake
Artist: Unsigned
Material: Ivory
Date: Twentieth century
Size: 1 3/4" x 1 1/2" x 1"

In one classical Japanese tale, court poet Ariwara no Narihira was travel-
ing from Kyoto to the northeastern province of Michinoku, and took lodg-
ing one night in a place called Ichiwarano. While resting, he heard the
upper triplet of a *tanka* being carried by the wind over the moor:

> The autumn wind—
> Each time it blows, the pain;
> The holes that once were eyes!

When he went out to see who was reciting the poem, he found only a skull
with pampas grass growing through the eyes. Each time the wind caused
the grass to sway, he heard the lines of the poem.

He then remembered another, similar poem, by an earlier poet, Ono no
Komachi, a great beauty and a great poet whose works were unsurpassed
in their elegance:

> In the autumn wind
> Your empty promises to meet me lie scattered
> Like lonely ears of grain,
> Painfully reminding me that I, too,
> Will remain unharvested.

Realizing that the voice he had heard must have been the spirit of Komachi
speaking to him, he said a prayer for the repose of her soul and completed
the poem she had begun with this couplet:

> No longer can I be called a small field *(ono)*,
> Just a moor where only pampas grass grows.

Plate 62

Subject: Japanese Ladies
Artist: Ryosei
Material: Ivory
Date: Late twentieth century
Size: Largest one, 2" high

We often find cross-cultural similarities when studying netsuke as a source of information about Japanese life and legend. The three ladies shown here are all by the same carver, Ryosei. They are seen in front of the palanquin of a powerful lord, as can be seen by the beauty of his carriage.

The palanquin itself is from an Imperial doll's set of furniture. It is shown on only one day of the year, March 3, as a special feature in the home. Many Imperial doll sets were sold for export over the past 30 years. Recently however, the popularity of them has grown as the Japanese economy has allowed some people to buy larger houses.

The Imperial doll sets contain the Emperor and Empress dolls that are placed on the top tier of shelving, and many attendants and accessories that are placed on the layers of shelving below them. Doll sets come in sizes to fit many different pocketbooks, so the elaborateness of the decoration varies, as well as the number of attendants, furniture, etc. Every set includes small offertory tables where special rice cakes and other foods are placed on this day honoring the girls in the household.

The doll's palanquin and the three netsuke Japanese ladies make the strong connection with Girls' Day for anyone who has been in Japan at the beginning of May. However, the first reaction that many others have to this image is to whistle or hum a tune from *The Mikado*, "Three Little Maids From School Are We," by Gilbert and Sullivan.

Ryosei, born Isamu Yabe in 1932, is a contemporary carver who enjoys re-creating the elegant costumes and beautiful ladies of the Edo period. His elaborate carving and meticuous lacquerwork are techniques well suited to his subjects. Some pieces are enhanced with a sprinkling of gold dust.

Plate 63

Subject: Buddha's-Hand Citron
Artist: Kyusai
Material: Wood
Date: Late nineteenth century
Size: 2 5/8" x 2 5/8" x 1 1/4"

The citron melon *(Citrus sarcodactylis)* is called the Buddha's-hand citron due to its shape. It is frequently carved in jade and other precious materials. This one is carved in wood.

A famous tale concerning a Buddha's-hand citron goes like this. Long ago, the famous warrior Yoshiie, the noted soothsayer Abe no Seimei, the esteemed doctor Tadaakira, and the holy priest Kanju all happened to be visiting the regent, Fujiwara no Michinaga. Early on the same day, a basket of fruit had been sent as a gift from the temples in Nara, but since it was a day of fasting at the palace, the gift was regarded with great suspicion. Abe no Seimei, asked to make a reading, declared that one of the melons contained poison. Kanju then started chanting over the fruits, and one of them began to jump up and down.

As that was judged to be the poisonous one, Tadaakira took two of his acupuncture needles and stuck them in the fruit to draw out the poison. At that, the fruit stopped jumping. Then Yoshiie suddenly drew his sword and cut the melon open. Inside they found a small poisonous snake, its head severed by Yoshiie's sword and its eyes pierced by the physician's needles.

Although Kyusai (1879-1938) worked mostly in ivory, this example and many others that are illustrated in books on netsuke are carved from wood. His subjects included natural objects such as mushrooms, bats, foxes, and cicadas, as well as man-made objects such as roof-tiles. Like Gyokuso (Plate 38), and some other netsuke carvers, the *himotoshi,* or passage-way for the cord, was often created out of a natural open area of the netsuke.

Plate 64

Subject: Kinko Riding a Carp
Artist: Yosei
Material: Ivory
Date: Twentieth century
Size: 1 3/4" x 1 5/8" x 1 3/8"

On the birth of his only son, K'ung-tzu (Confucius) received a gift of some carp from the ruler of the state of Lu, Duke Chao; in honor of the gift, he named his son K'ung Li (*li* means carp). The carp has long been revered in the Orient as a symbol of strength and perseverance. Why was this fish who lives in muddy waters and lives off the refuse at the bottom, much like the catfish, chosen to symbolize strength of will? The Chinese classics relate the legend that each year on the third day of the third month, the carp ascend the mighty Yellow River, fighting their way through the cataracts, and leaping over the Dragon Gate; it was believed that those that succeeded in passing through were instantly transformed into dragons.

The fortitude of the carp is still celebrated in Japan on Boys' Day (May 5), when *koi nobori,* or streamers shaped like carp, are attached to long poles, from where they fly over the rooftops of the houses of families having sons, in the hope that the boys will grow up to be as strong and perseverant as the carp endeavoring to become dragons. Since they are incipient dragons, carp are almost always portrayed in Chinese and Japanese art as horned or with great whiskers, which often causes them to be mistaken for catfish by Western viewers.

A Taoist hermit named Kinko was a skilled lutist and a excellent painter of fishes, who lived beside a river. One day when he was bathing, a great carp appeared and offered to take him into the river realm for a short time. After about a month, he returned, riding upon the back of the King of the Fishes. After begging his disciples never to kill any more fish, he dove into the river and was never seen again, having been transformed into a carp himself!

He is usually portrayed, as in this netsuke, as a smiling old man, often holding a scroll in one hand and a wine gourd in the other, seated on the back of a large carp having long whiskers or horns.

Plate 65

Subject: Kunimitsu
Artist: Kunimitsu
Material: Ivory
Date: Mid-twentieth century

These four netsuke are all by the same artist—Kunimitsu. It is no wonder that they all look similar, because each netsuke is a miniature portrait of the artist. Even though the head is only one-quarter of an inch tall, you can actually see the artist age by looking at netsuke from different periods in his career. Of course, the receding hair line is constant, because that is the style that was used in feudal Japan, when craftsmen would be seen dressed in these traditional robes. Most of Kunimitsu's netsuke are so intricately carved that they would be damaged if they were ever worn in the traditional manner. They are reminiscent of the *oki*-netsuke that were created to please the eye rather than for practical usage. Kunimitsu was born in the 1920s and was an active carver until 1984.

Plate 66

Subject: Reclining Figure Reading a Handscroll
Artist: Mitsutoshi
Material: Ivory
Date: Late nineteenth century
Size: 1 3/8" x 15/16" x 15/16"

The best-known handscroll in the West is the Torah. The Chinese and Japanese have also used the handscroll for centuries, as a sort of magic carpet. Most subjects rendered on handscrolls were things that could not be studied in one glance. One favorite theme is a river boat journey, where many miles of countryside are shown. Other paintings show royal processions, battles, a compilation of famous mountains, panoramas of towns, and the changing seasons.

When handscrolls are displayed at museums, they are often stretched out their full length and shown in a case under glass. The figure in this netsuke is showing us the proper way to view a handscroll—a few inches at a time. It may be done alone or with one or two friends. The next time that you encounter a handscroll in a museum, take the time to inspect it closely. Look at a section of it that is only six inches wide. Then move along the scroll, carefully observing the next section and then the next. Enjoy the details. See the little person on the boat. Smell the ocean spray, and listen to the waterfall.

Born Otani Koga, Mitsutoshi (fl. late nineteenth century) specialized in carving figures in ivory. He lived in the Asakusa area of Tokyo, along the Sumida River.

Plate 67

Inro
Subject: Waterfront Cottage
Artist: Jokasai
Material: Lacquer
Date: Late seventeenth century
Size: 2" x 1 7/8" x 5/8"

Many aspects of traditional Japanese architecture are fascinating to Westerners. One of the reasons is the eloquent use of natural materials. The roof of this waterfront cottage is held up with natural, unfinished tree trunks. The idea is to harmonize the building with nature. It is not a sign of impoverishment, as the same technique is used in many buildings owned by the Imperial family, including the very famous tea house at the Katsura Imperial Villa in Kyoto.

The roof is natural thatch, a technique that has been used in almost every country that has suitable materials. A thatch roof lasts for 50 years or more, therefore this is a fairly old house, as we can see the roof support through the thatch. And through the poles holding up the roof, we can see the traditional *shoji*, or panels made of lightweight wood and paper that slide past one another to allow the breeze off of the pond into the house. The traditional interior of a house like this was open and had a light feeling to it because the *shoji* paper is translucent, allowing light into the interior while preventing viewers from seeing in.

The *ojime* is carved from coral, and the netsuke itself is another example of the lacquerer's skill.

An outstanding lacquerer, Jokasai received a large order for *inro* and *kogo* from the Tokugawa family in 1682. To complete the order, he and Koami Nagafusa joined forces, and all of their pupils worked diligently to help complete the work. The Koami family were lacquerers to the court from the early fifteenth to the twentieth century. Followers of Jokasai continued to work for the shogunate until the Meiji Restoration in 1868.

Plate 68

The opposite side of the *inro* shown in Plate 67

Many *inro* have similar scenes on each side, such as the cranes flying and alighting on the Frontispiece and in Plate 72, or the three Dutchmen on the following *inro*. Another approach is to create a single scene going around the piece. Here, the herons are in a natural extension of the scenery around the waterfront cottage seen in Plate 67.

One heron legend tells of an evening party being held by Emperor Daigo. He saw a heron in one corner of the Shinsen Imperial garden and sent an attendant to catch it. When the bird started to fly away, the attendant called to the bird, saying, "It is the august command of His Imperial Majesty that you appear before him and not fly off." The bird stood still and was caught and taken to the Emperor. The Emperor was so pleased with such a beautiful bird that he appointed it to the fifth court rank. Henceforth, the black-crowned night heron has been known as *goi-sagi,* or "fifth-rank heron." The story is continually retold in the popular Noh drama, *Sagi.*

Plate 69

Inro
Subject: Foreigners
Artist: Shujosai
Material: Lacquer
Date: ca. 1900
Size: 3 1/2" x 1 13/16" x 1 1/16"

Fernando Mendez Pinto was the first European to set foot in Japan. A Portuguese navigator in the early sixteenth century, he arrived there sometime around 1545. He had traveled in India, China and Japan before returning to Lisbon in 1550 to settle down. The ships that then visited the Japanese ports were highly ornamented with bow and stern carvings. The netsuke that were produced showing Dutchmen were generally inspired by these carvings. There are examples of these ship's carvings in the collections of Japanese nobility of the period.

In eighteenth-century Japan, Europeans were described as "imaginary beings with cat's eyes, huge noses, red hair, and shrike's tongues." The Dutch merchants were confined to the Island of Dejima in Nagasaki harbor. Once a year, the representative of the Dutch East India Company was allowed to visit the Shogun in Edo (present-day Tokyo), thus affording the only possible glimpse of these "southern barbarians."

(See overleaf for both sides of this beautiful inro *and the interesting* manju-*style netsuke attached to it.)*

Plate 71

Subject: Daruma Doll, Drum, Okame Mask, Daikoku's Mallet
Artist: Gyokkosai
Material: Ivory
Date: Mid-nineteenth century
Size: 1 7/8" x 1 1/4" x 7/8"

In a paperback book titled *Festivals of Japan,* there is a listing for a festival, somewhere in Japan, for almost every day of the year. Some of them are esoteric, such as the "Seven Laughing Men," that is held each year in Tokyo. Another is the *Sagi-mai* or "Dance of the Spirit of the Herons," which takes place each year on July 17 at the Yasaka Shrine in Kyoto.

Others Japanese festivals are becoming well-known in the west, such as the Kite Battle festivals held in various locations in the spring; Boys' Day *(Tango no Sekku)* when carp-shaped banners (*koi nobori*) are flown, on May 5; and *Gion Matsuri* in Kyoto, for the month of July.

This netsuke seems to combine the spirit of every festival in Japan. It contains a drum, a Daruma doll, Daikoku's mallet, and an Okame mask. Festivals, or *matsuri,* are occasions similar to Mardi-Gras in the west, where nearly everyone participates. Someone who is shy might put on the Okame mask and let their inhibitions go while dancing and singing in their Okame disguise. Another reveler may choose to urge on the occasion by beating a drum. The Daruma doll, as we have already discovered, is a talisman of good luck---for a new venture and the new year; while Daikoku's mallet is a symbol of wealth.

Thus, this unpretentious ivory netsuke symbolizes good times, good luck, and continuing prosperity throughout the entire year. It also serves to remind us once again that netsuke provide an endless treasure of information, entertainment, and enjoyment to all who fondle and inspect them, whether first-hand or vicariously through books such as this one.

Gyokkosai (fl. 1830--67) was extremely proficient at carving netsuke of human figures, animals and masks.

Plate 72

Netsuke, *Ojime,* and *Inro* on a Theme of Longevity.

Netsuke
Subject: Japanese crane
Artist: Shingetsu
Material: Ivory with lacquer
Date: Late twentieth century
Size: 1 3/4" x 1 1/4" x 7/8"

Ojime
Subject: Chrysanthemums
Artist: Unsigned
Material: Ivory
Date: Nineteenth century
Size: 5/8" diameter

Inro
Subject: Cranes
Artist: Hyakusen
Material: Lacquer
Date: Late eighteenth century
Size: 3 3/8" x 2 1/8" x 3/4"

This combination of netsuke, *ojime*, and *inro* makes an interesting group that would be excellent for a contemporary Japanese gentleman to wear. They show a knowledge of the past and an interest in encouraging contemporary artists to continue a traditional art. The symbology of the crane is well known to you now. The chrysanthemum is a plant-world equivalent to the crane, as it blossoms in the fall and is also a symbol of longevity.

Chrysanthemums have been cultivated in China and Japan for thousands of years. A special chrysanthemum-viewing party was first held in Japan on the ninth day of the ninth month of 685. The occasion was so special that Emperor Tenmu attended the party and every guest was given a special gift to commemorate the occasion.

This illustration culminates the essence of what we have been learning throughout *Netsuke: Japanese Life and Legend in Miniature.* It appropriately closes our visit to the customs and culture of Japan for this time. The opposite side of this *inro* shows the cranes as they are landing to settle down for the evening (and study some interesting folktales about people that they will eventually relate to their children). I have chosen this side of the *inro* to close the book, because it symbolizes the flights of imagination that anyone can travel on while viewing netsuke, once they have learned some of the intriguing stories that are revealed about Japanese life and legends in these fascinating, miniature, sculptural works of art.

Selected Bibliography

Allen, Maude Rex. *Japanese Art Motives.* Chicago: A.C. McClurg, 1917.

Arakawa, Hirokazu (Tokyo National Museum). *The Go Collection of Netsuke.* Tokyo and New York: Kodansha International.

Bush, Lewis. *Japanalia, Past and Present.* In two volumes. Tokyo: The Japan Times, 1967.

Bushell, Raymond. *Collector's Netsuke.* New York and Tokyo: John Weatherhill, 1975.

_____. *An Introduction to Netsuke.* Tokyo and Rutland, Vermont: Charles E. Tuttle, 1971.

_____. *The Wonderful World of Netsuke.* Tokyo and Rutland, Vermont: Charles E. Tuttle, 1964.

Davey, Neil K. *Netsuke.* London: Faber & Faber, 1974, in association with Sotheby, Parke Bernet Publications.

Davis, F. Hedland. *Myths and Legends of Japan.* London: Harrop, 1912.

Dorson, Richard M. *Folk Legends of Japan.* Tokyo and Rutland, Vermont: Charles E. Tuttle, 1962.

Edmunds, Will H. *Pointers and Clues to the Subjects of Chinese and Japanese Art.* London: Sampson Low, Marston, 1934.

Forman, Werner: *Japanese Netsuke.* London: Spring Books, 1960.

Hurtig, Bernard, compiler: *Masterpieces of Netsuke Art: One Thousand Favorites of Leading Collectors.* New York and Tokyo: John Weatherhill, 1973 (published for the International Netsuke Collectors' Society).

_____. *Rare Netsuke Masterpieces.* Honolulu: Orientwest, n.d.

_____. *Journal of The International Netsuke Collectors Society.* Honolulu: International Netsuke Collectors Society, 1977–85.

Jahss, Melvin, and Jahss, Betty. *Inro and Other Miniature Forms of Japanese Lacquer Art.* Tokyo and Rutland, Vermont: Charles E. Tuttle, 1971.

Japan Netsuke Carvers' Association. *Exhibition of Contemporary Netsuke 1982; 1983; 1984; 1985; 1986; 1987; 1988.* Tokyo: Japan Netsuke Carvers' Association.

Japan Travel Bureau. *Festivals of Japan.* Tokyo: Japan Travel Bureau, 1987.

Joly, Henri L. *Legend in Japanese Art.* Tokyo and Rutland, Vermont: Charles E. Tuttle, 1967.

Joya, Mock. *Quaint Customs & Manners of Japan.* In three volumes. Tokyo: Tokyo News Service, 1953.

Jonas, F. M. *Netsuke*. London: Kegan Paul, Trench, Trubman, 1928; reprinted by Tokyo and Rutland, Vermont: Charles E. Tuttle, 1960.

Kinsey, Miriam. *Contemporary Netsuke*. Tokyo and Rutland, Vermont: Charles E. Tuttle, 1977.

———. *Living Masters of Netsuke*. Tokyo and New York: Kodansha International, 1983.

Lazarnick, George. *The Signature Book of Netsuke, Inro and Ojime Artists in Photographs*. Honolulu: Reed Publishers, 1976.

London Netsuke Committee. *Contrasting Styles*. London: Sawers, 1980.

Mitford, A.B. (Lord Redesdale). *Tales of Old Japan*. Tokyo and Rutland, Vermont: Charles E. Tuttle, 1966.

Moss, Paul. *Japanese Netsuke: Serious Art*. London: Sydney L. Moss, 1989.

Naito, Hiroshi. *Legends of Japan*. Tokyo and Rutland, Vermont: Charles E. Tuttle, 1972.

Netsuke Kenkyukai Society. *Netsuke Kenkyukai Study Journal*. Torrance, CA: Netsuke Kenkyukai Society.

O'Brien, Mary Louise. *Netsuke: A guide for Collectors*. Tokyo and Rutland, Vermont: Charles E. Tuttle, 1965.

Reikichi, Ueda. *The Netsuke Handbook of Ueda Reikichi*. Adapted from the Japanese by Raymond Bushell. Tokyo and Rutland, Vermont: Charles E. Tuttle, 1961.

Roberts, Laurance P. *A Dictionary of Japanese Artists*. New York and Tokyo: John Weatherhill, 1976.

Ryerson, Egerton. *The Netsuke of Japan*. London: G. Bell and Sons, 1958.

Sakade, Florence. *Little One-Inch and Other Japanese Children's Favorite Stories*. Tokyo and Rutland, Vermont: Charles E. Tuttle, 1958.

Shimizu, Yoshiaki. *Japan: The Shaping of Daimyo Culture, 1185--1868*. Washington, D.C.: National Gallery of Art, 1988.

Sunatomo, Seiichiro. *Exhibition of Fine Contemporary Netsuke*. Tokyo: Sunatomo Co., 1989.

Symmes, Edwin and Symmes, Rhena. *Native Treasures: American Bonsai Photo Book*. Atlanta, Georgia: E. C. Symmes Associates, 1973.

Takama, Shinji. *The World of Bamboo*. South San Francisco: Heian, 1981.

Tokyo National Museum. *Special Exhibition, Art of the Muromachi Period*. Tokyo: Tokyo National Museum, 1989.

Tsukamoto, Takumi. *Folk Legends of Aso*. Kumamoto: Takumi Tsukamoto, 1985.

Tollner, Madeline R. *Netsuke*. San Francisco: Academy Phototype Service, 1954. Second printing, San Francisco: Fearon Publishers, 1960.

Williams, C.A.S. *Chinese Symbolism and Art Motifs.* Shanghai: Kelly and Walsh, 1941; reprinted Tokyo and Rutland, Vermont: Charles E. Tuttle, 1965.

Yamaguchi, H.S.K. *We Japanese*. Hakone: Fujiya Hotel, 1949.

Yanagita, Kunio. *Japanese Folk Tales*. Translated by Fanny Hagin Mayer. Tokyo: Tokyo News Service, 1954; second edition, 1958.

Yasuda, Yuri: *Old Tales of Japan*. Tokyo and Rutland, Vermont: Charles E. Tuttle, 1953.

Glossary-Index

foreigners, 185
fox (*kitsune*), 172
frog (*kaeru*), 76, 148, 170
Fujiwara no Michinaga (area ruler), 176
Fukazawa (village), 104

Gama Sennin (Toad Sage), 148
Ganbun (carver), 86
ghosts, 172
ginkgo nut, 70
Gion Matsuri (Kyoto festival), 188
Girls' Day (March 3), 174
God of Calligraphy (Tenjin-sama), 110
God of Wealth (Daikoku), 112
God of the Underworld (Emma-O), 112
Goddess of Mercy (Kannon), 102
Goddess of Mirth (Okame), 108
goi-sagi (black-crowned night heron), 184
gold, use of, 37
Golden Pavilion (Kyoto), 58
gourd, 54, 128
Grand Shrine of Ise, 160
Grus japonensis (Japanese crane), 140
Gyokkosai (carver), 188
Gyokudo (carver), 60
Gyokukan (carver), 60
Gyokusho (carver), 60
Gyokuso (carver), 128, 176
Gyokuzan (carver), 104

Hachiko (famous loyal dog), 144
haiku (17-syllable poem), 14
handscroll, 180
hara-tsuzumi (*tanuki*), 72
heron, 184
Hidemasa (carver), 120
Hideyuki (carver), 130
hikime (humming-bulb head for arrow), 168
himotoshi (cord holes), 26, 27
hippopotamus, 28, 32, 34, 36
Hirado porcelain, 122, 124
Hitachi Province, 178
hoe, 94
Hojitsu (carver), 62
Hokkaido (northernmost main island), 132, 155
Hokusai (ukiyo-e artist), 132
Horai (sacred mountain), 140
horn, 32
Hui Shih (ancient Chinese ruler), 36
Humming-Bulb-Arrow Ceremony, 168
hunter, 72, 82, 140
Hyakusen (lacquerer), 190

Ichiwarano, 172
Ikkan (carver), 78
immortality, 150

Imperial doll set, 168, 174
Imperial Palace, 162
Imperial Palace in China, 160
incense box (*kogo*), 160
inro, 24, 26, 27, 29, 54, 182, 184, 185, 190
International Netsuke Carvers' Association, 33, 36
Inu-dera (Dog Temple), 126
Inu-Kubo (Dog Prince), 126
Ittan (carver), 134
ivory, 32, 34, 37
Iwami School (featured natural scenes), 44, 64

Japan Ivory Carvers' Association, 170
Japan Netsuke Carvers' Association, 33
Japanese archery (*kyudo*), 76, 168
Japanese badger (*tanuki*), 72
Japanese Ladies (Ryosei), 174
Japanese wood-block prints (ukiyo-e), 162
J panese wrestling (sumo), 106
jellyfish, 84, 116
Jokasai (lacquerer), 27, 182
judo, 106
Jugyoku (carver), 110, 166

Kabuki (theater), 13, 122, 148
kagami-buta (flat, discshaped netsuke), 37, 146
Kaigyokusai (carver), 54
Kangyoku (carver), 62, 72, 114
Kanju (holy priest), 176
Kannon (Japanese name of Kuan-yin, goddess of mercy), 102
kappa (mythical creature), 62
karate, 106
Katsura Imperial Villa (Kyoto), 182
Keisai (carver), 58
Kenji (carver), 68
kimono, 25, 44, 54, 140
Kinko (Ch'in Kao), 178
Kintaro (legendary mountain boy), 82
kirin (mythical benevolent creature), 62, 138
Kitashirakawa, HIH Prince Yoshihisa of, 104
Kite Battle, 188
Koami Nagafusa (lacquerer), 182
Koetsu (carver), 170
kogo (incense box), 160, 182
Kogyokyu (carver), 142
Kumamoto (city on Kyushu island), 19
Kumamoto Handicrafts Center, 37
K'ung Li (Confucius' son), 178
K'ung-tzu (Confucius), 178
Kunimitsu (carver), 88, 118, 180
Kuan-yin (Chinese name of Kannon), 102
Kyogen (theater), 13, 136